READING IS OUR BUSINESS

How Libraries Can Foster
Reading Comprehension

Sharon Grimes

American Library Association
Chicago
2006

Printed on 50-pound white offset, a pH-neutral stock, and bound in 10-point C1S cover stock by McNaughton & Gunn.

The paper used in this publication meets the minimum requirements of American National Standard for Information Sciences—Permanence of Paper for Printed Library Materials, ANSI Z39.48-1992. ∞

Library of Congress Cataloging-in-Publication Data

Grimes, Sharon.
    Reading is our business : how libraries can foster reading comprehension / Sharon Grimes.
       p.   cm.
    Includes bibliographical references and index.
    ISBN 0-8389-0912-4
    1. School libraries—Activity programs—United States. 2. Reading comprehension—Study and teaching (Elementary)—United States. I. Title.
    Z675.S3G74 2006
    027.80973—dc22   2005028263

Printed in the United States of America

10   09   08   07   06   5   4   3   2   1

*In loving memory of
Chelsey Weigman,
granddaughter extraordinaire
and grandma's best reader.
Save some books
for us to read together
in that great library
in the sky.*

Contents

Preface

It's troubling to witness the duality of the reading and library communities, with literacy being the neglected common ground on which few reading experts and librarians dare to tread collaboratively.

Evan St. Lifer, "Parallel Universes"

Reading Is Our Business attempts to cultivate literacy and encourage library media specialists to resume or assume (depending on whom you are talking to) their rightful position as critical partners in the development of reading comprehension. Its intent is to transform and inform how and for whom we

- share storytime,
- create and conduct book clubs, whether virtual or real time, and
- change the ways we display, recommend, and talk about books.

This book is based on my experiences as a school library media specialist at Lansdowne Elementary, as well as the discoveries of my fellow teachers, intrepid explorers on the path to improve reading comprehension for every student. Lansdowne Elementary is a Title I school located in Baltimore County, Maryland. Our biggest challenge is the impact of poverty. Of the school's total enrollment, 61 percent qualify for free or reduced lunch (43 percent on free lunch; 18 percent on reduced lunch). The majority of our children are not prepared to begin school because they lack phonemic and print awareness. In addition, many come to us with severe language and experiential deficits that place them far behind their more affluent peers. Similarly, many of their parents are not prepared to help them with the support and guidance to sustain and further develop the skills taught in school. Thirty-four percent of our parents had their first child when they were teenagers. Our parents care deeply about their children but, as a result of their youth and economic circumstances, lack many of the skills necessary to become full partners in developing their children's literacy. According to the National Research Council's (1998) Committee on the Prevention of Reading Difficulties in Young Children, demographic data suggest that most reading problems tend to occur in children from poor families with little education. Sixty-one percent of our kindergarten parents do not participate in our independent reading program that asks parents to read to and with their child for a minimum of fifteen minutes a night, suggesting that the majority of kindergarten students are seldom read to by an adult or older child.

There are three critical components to reading: print awareness, the ability to decode (including phonemic and phonological awareness), and the ability to comprehend. Direct instruction has enabled many of our students to become proficient decoders and develop print awareness; they can read the words and turn the pages, but they do not understand what they read. We know that proficient readers think about reading; they have an ongoing dialogue with the text before they begin reading, during reading, and after reading. This dialogue with the text is a learned behavior. Good readers have had it modeled for them from birth and know what conversations with text look and sound like. When this modeling is absent or incomplete, teachers, reading specialists, and yes, librarians, both school and public, must fill the gap.

Reading Is Our Business intends to bridge this critical gap by providing a practical how-to guide for teaching comprehension strategies in school and public libraries. Chapters 2 through 9 explain individual reading comprehension strategies and illustrate how you can teach them in your library. Appendixes contain suggested titles for each of the strategies and other resources for supporting strategy instruction. Additionally, each chapter builds on a theoretical framework by summarizing current research. Seminal works that have influenced my thinking and practice include the following:

> *Teaching Children to Read: An Evidence-Based Assessment of the Scientific Research Literature on Reading and Its Implications for Reading Instruction* (NICHD 2000)
>
> *Mosaic of Thought: Teaching Comprehension in a Reader's Workshop* (Keene and Zimmermann 1997)
>
> *7 Keys to Comprehension* (Zimmermann and Hutchins 2003)

Strategies That Work: Teaching Comprehension to Enhance Understanding (Harvey and Goudvis 2000)

Beyond Technology: Questioning, Research and the Information Literate School (McKenzie 2000)

Reading with Meaning: Teaching Comprehension in the Primary Grades (Miller 2002)

Acknowledgments

This book would not have been possible without the pioneering work of extraordinary teachers and staff developers at the Denver-based Public Education and Business Coalition, especially Debbie Miller, who first suggested that I write a book about the important role library media specialists have in teaching comprehension strategies. The support of my family, friends, students, colleagues, library media supervisor, and school principal was equally indispensable. My husband, Jim, cooked, cleaned, and washed clothes to help me make time for writing. More important, he seemed to intuit when I needed advice, encouragement, or just a break from writing. My two still-at-home children, Beth and Ryan, patiently suffered through my bouts of grumpiness, always encouraged me to follow my dreams, and actually seemed to enjoy that I was too distracted to pry into every aspect of their lives! Their friend Chrissy also cleaned, learned to cook, and even alphabetized the many book suggestions. My grandson Eric actually learned to make his own grilled cheese and offered countless suggestions about the importance of reading.

I feel very blessed to work with the truly outstanding teachers and amazing staff at Lansdowne Elementary School in Baltimore County, Maryland. Three years ago, we began studying how to change the way we taught reading. We already knew why we wanted to transform reading: our wonderful students, whom I want to thank for sharing their thinking, suggestions, and growing excitement about reading. Teachers read numerous books and articles, participated in lengthy faculty meetings, and supported each other as we began to transform how we taught reading. They willingly shared ideas, teaching suggestions, sympathetic ears, and a shoulder to cry on as needed. I especially want to thank the brave teachers who took my action research course on teaching reading comprehension strategies: Rachael Gardner, Kim Grant, Leesa Green, Katie Gross, Laurie Okun, Jessica Petree, Kathy Powell, Kelly Veloso, and Barbara Zink. Together, we discovered how to use the rubric I designed to effectively assess the evidence of students' thinking and build a professional learning community. The statistics about student growth presented in this book were gathered by these intrepid teachers, who let neither the difficulty of our task nor the many challenges we faced deter them. I want to extend a special thanks to Leesa Green, who read numerous drafts and provided countless suggestions for improvement. And I will never be able to express fully my appreciation to Rita Wells, my library aide, who works six to seven hours every day even though she is paid for only three; she single-handedly ran our reading programs while I wrote the book.

None of this would have been possible, however, without the impetus provided by our dynamic principal, Anne Gold. It was Anne who first read about the work of the Denver-based Public Education and Business Coalition; she not only encouraged us to read *Strategies That Work: Teaching Comprehension to Enhance Understanding* but bought each of us a copy. When the staff expressed doubts about how comprehension strategies could be taught in the primary grades, she not only purchased for us Debbie Miller's book, *Reading with Meaning: Teaching Comprehension in the Primary Grades*, but also found a way to bring Miller to our school so that she could model teaching comprehension strategies with our students. Anne's support of reading is exceeded only by her determination to provide the very best for our students.

Without the support and encouragement of Della Curtis, my library media supervisor, the article "The Search for Meaning" (Grimes 2004), which was the catalyst for this book, would not have appeared in *School Library Journal*. And without her foresight and leadership abilities I would not have been able to make the transition from high school English teacher to elementary school library media specialist. Among the many amazing collaborations she has forged, the one that most influenced me is the innovative cohort program she developed with Towson University to train outstanding classroom teachers to become school librarians.

Finally, I want to acknowledge the contributions of Chelsey Weigman, whose love of reading and untimely death inspired me, her grandmother, to sow the joy of reading and the ability to comprehend in every child I meet.

1
The Invitation

If you are a dreamer, come in,
If you are a dreamer, a wisher, a liar,
A hope-er, a pray-er, a magic
bean buyer . . .

Shel Silverstein,
"Invitation"

*I*magine. Second-grade students, newly emergent readers, lined up out-side of your door with their library books clutched in their hands as though those books were their most prized possessions. Then, look closely at each book; each is covered with sticky notes, tangible evidence of stu-dents thinking, connecting, visualizing, questioning, and making meaning of the text. Visualize a sea full of hands eagerly waving, each student wait-ing to share his or her connection, question, mind-movie, prediction, infer-ence, or synthesis. But you don't have to imagine it. Teaching your library customers how to become active readers who employ strategies to make meaning from any text will transform your library and every reader who enters your door.

That this transformation is desperately needed is demonstrated by a national trend of decreasing comprehension scores and by circulation sta-tistics that vary widely according to the socioeconomic status of the com-munity serviced. Marlene Asselin warns, "The harsh news for both teachers and teacher-librarians is that free reading is not enough to ensure optimal development of comprehension abilities" (2002, 55). Not only is it not enough to provide equitable access to resources or to wish that our clients were better readers, but also we cannot afford to ignore the social implications of comprehension scores and circulation statistics that are directly related to socioeconomic status. Nor can we continue to delegate the development of comprehension to reading specialists. Literacy cannot be the "neglected common ground" between library media and reading specialists if we are to have readers into the twenty-first century and beyond (St. Lifer 2004).

Why librarians? We already do some of that, and anyway, don't we have enough to do already? These are just a few of the comments I can almost hear my colleagues making. They are absolutely right. Public and school librarians do, through storytimes, develop print awareness and decoding skills, but we need to expand our efforts in the critical area of developing comprehension. Providing access to wonderful books is not enough. Children cannot come to value what they do not comprehend. Modeling enjoyment of reading is also not sufficient; children will not enjoy what they do not understand. Storytime, no matter how entertaining or well planned, does not increase the participants' comprehension skills.

Only comprehension instruction will allow children to access the treasure trove of all that was and will ever be. As the National Reading Panel reports, when readers are given instruction on how to think about and have an ongoing dialogue with the text,

> They make significant gains on measures of reading comprehension over students trained with conventional instruction. Teaching a variety of reading comprehension strategies in natural settings and content areas leads to increased learning of the strategies, to specific transfer of learning, to increased memory and understanding of new passages, and, in some cases to general improvements in comprehension. Students show noticeable improvement on standardized tests. More intensive instruction and modeling have been more successful in improving reading and standardized test scores. (NICHD 2000)

What setting is more natural for reading than the library?

The effects of comprehension instruction conducted in natural settings, like the library, are even more noticeable for readers who begin instruction labeled as poor readers. Research shows that

> [in] studies involving even a few hours of preparation, instructors taught students who were poor readers but adequate decoders to apply various strategies to expository texts in reading groups, with a teacher demonstrating, guiding, or modeling the strategies, and with teacher scaffolding.

Even limited use of these strategies produced noticeable improvement in their use by students. (NICHD 2000)

One of the most exciting results of this body of research is that comprehension strategy instruction was found to be especially effective for students who began the study as able decoders but poor comprehenders—probably because they were less likely to invent effective strategies on their own. In some studies, when less able readers who had been taught a comprehension strategy were assessed on their performance of the strategy, they were indistinguishable from more able readers who had not been taught the strategy directly (NICHD 2000).

Teaching comprehension strategies means teaching readers how to become actively engaged with the text, which is particularly important for readers who come from a low socioeconomic background. As Topping et al. (2003) report, "In our increasingly diverse student populations, supporting reading engagement is especially important as the effect of high engagement can mitigate effects of SES [socioeconomic status]." Active readers are engaged readers; they actively employ the strategies that decades of research show proficient readers use, such as these:

Previewing. Good readers use a variety of strategies to preview and select a "just right" text.

Connecting. Effective readers use what they know to understand what they read by connecting the text to their personal experiences, their prior experiences with other texts, and their knowledge of world events and history.

Questioning. Good readers ask questions and look for answers before, during, and after reading. They ask themselves questions like, "Why did the author choose those details?" or "Why did that character act that way?"

Visualizing. Proficient readers create visual images as they read. They can picture and even draw the characters, settings, and events in a story.

Inferring. Good readers infer when the author does not answer their questions directly. You frequently hear them say, "I think this means . . . ," or "I can tell by the character's actions that she must feel. . . ."

Predicting. Excellent readers guess what happens next based on clues in the text.

Synthesizing. Proficient readers combine what they know with new information to understand the text.

Determining important ideas. Good readers understand the main ideas and the author's message because they ask themselves constantly as they read, "What is the author trying to tell us?"

Applying "fix-up strategies." Thoughtful readers use all of the above comprehension strategies *and* fix-up strategies, like using context clues to define words, rereading to clarify meaning, and using questions and connections to make meaning.

The problem with the above listing of strategies is that it suggests a linear progression, whereas the reality is recursive; readers can and should reflect, share, evaluate, and begin to apply knowledge during reading. Students can and do continue to connect, visualize, synthesize, and so forth after reading if the text is a meaningful one for them. Although as a teacher you will model each of these strategies as a discrete application, constantly remind yourself and your students that good readers employ each of these as their interactions with the text demand.

What does research tell us about the best way to teach these comprehension strategies? One group of studies examined the effects of teachers' modeling of cognitive strategies, like think-alouds and direct explanations, on students' comprehension abilities. After the teachers modeled the use of comprehension strategies, students were mentored as they used the new strategy until they were able to employ it independently. The increases in students' ability to understand the text were so dramatic that "the very concept of instruction was redefined from 'mentioning' [the strategies that should be used] to making concrete the mental and motivational processes used by proficient readers" (NICHD 2000).

Additional research by Fielding and Pearson (1994) supports the use of scaffolded instruction that begins with teacher modeling, through think-alouds, the strategies good readers use to access and create meaning. Fielding and Pearson suggest a four-step approach that includes teacher modeling, guided practice, independent practice, and application of the reading strategies in authentic reading situations. Further support for explicit modeling and the gradual release of responsibility to the students is provided by Vygotsky's (1978) early work on instruction within the zone of proximal development and scaffolding, which clearly showed the benefits of gradually relinquishing support as students became more competent.

What are the implications of the research for our day-to-day practice? Libraries have always appealed to the child who is "the dreamer" and "the magic bean buyer," but those children are, as we know, a small subgroup of the total population. There are many other types of learners for whom the art and science of reading must be made explicit through modeling; through multiple opportunities for guided and dependent practice; and finally through scaffolded independent application of the strategies research shows proficient readers use: previewing, connecting, questioning, visualizing, inferring, predicting, synthesizing, determining important ideas, and applying fix-up strategies.

Reading is an active process of constructing meaning; those who understand the process best—librarians, reading specialists, and teachers—must make explicit and active what good readers do subconsciously and internally. It is never enough to *tell* children what good readers do; you must first be explicit and say that you are modeling the behavior, and then model the behavior exactly as you want to see it practiced by the students. The next step is to ask students what they observed as you were modeling use of the strategy; this becomes the framework and checklist they use as they begin guided practice.

Guided practice is usually whole group instruction, because you are guiding and supporting students as they practice using the strategy. The next step for students is dependent practice, where they practice using the strategy, usually with a peer. Together, the students provide support for one another as they use the strategy while the teacher circulates to assess students' implementation of the strategy and to hold discussions with individual teams as to why and/or how the strategy helps them to become better readers. Throughout the process, constantly ask the students to reflect on these questions:

- What do good readers do?
- What do they look like?
- Where do they read?
- What do they read?
- Why do they read?
- How does use of this strategy make you a better reader?

Finally, and this usually takes anywhere from a week to a month, students are ready to begin using the strategy independently.

What does comprehension instruction look like in a school library? Students enter my library, books clutched in their hands, covered in sticky notes. In the hallway, they have listened to my instructions for the day; maybe today they need, in addition to finding that "just right" book, to get a clipboard, a handout or a pack of sticky notes, a pencil, and always a carpet square. I set the timer and students do one of three things:

> If they need a new library book, they use our rules for selecting a "just right" book from the library collection.

> If they plan to renew their library books, they find a comfortable place in our library to read. In addition to the couch and chairs, we have benches and a huge menagerie of stuffed toys. When the two-minute warning from the timer sounds, all of the students gather the supplies they need for the smart thinking we will do that day.

> Those few sad students (and the number dwindles as the year progresses) who have forgotten their library books get a book from the crate next to my rocker, and they too find a comfortable place to read. Many times these are my friends from the homeless shelter; they need the solace and comfort a good book brings even more than many of my other students, and, of course, they need a good book to use for their smart thinking activity.

Students who want to share their thinking put their sticky notes on our "Smart Thinking" board. During the first eight minutes, I examine the Smart Thinking board to see whose thinking I will highlight during share time, and I confer with students about either a book selection or some insight or question they had about their books.

When the timer rings, someone (in the beginning of the year it is me, but later this is one of many jobs that students assume responsibility for as the year progresses) pushes the "Play" button, and our gather song begins to play. By the time the song ends, students know they should have gathered all the materials they need for the day and be seated "crisscross applesauce" ready to begin.[1]

We begin by sharing the smart thinking we had during the week. Depending on the focus of the mini-modeling session that day, I either invite students to share or select a sticky note from the board and say, "Timmy had this really smart thought that I just have to share. Would you like me to read it aloud or would you like to?" Then I ask my audience, "What do you think makes that a really smart thought? How can it help us become better readers?" I might say, "That reminds me of another smart thought that Bethie had. Let's look at that." Or I might ask, "Can you explain a little bit more about what you were thinking when you wrote this?" Each question helps students clarify the cognitive process of reading.

Next I review the objective for the day: "Today we will make text-to-self connections in guided practice." Then I always talk about what the strategy is, why the strategy is important, and how good readers use it to become even better readers. Because this is elementary school, I almost always have a visual, usually a poster that contains a definition and graphics so that even my non-readers can begin to conceptualize the strategy. Because the poster is next to the Smart Thinking board, students have already begun to think about the strategy before I begin talking. The first time I introduce a strategy, I use a think-aloud. When students are ready for the next stage, I choose a student and together we model what it looks like in dependent practice. When the students' thinking demonstrates that they are ready to apply the strategy independently, I might have a student model what it would look like in independent practice.

Students then have a block of time to apply the strategy in guided, dependent, or independent practice. Frequently they spread throughout the library, one student choosing a quiet corner, another a table. As students work, I call each one up as quietly and unobtrusively as possible to check books in or out *and* to have discussions with each student about what they are thinking.

Finally, we end each library session—all of us gathered together again—by sharing what we wrote down about what we learned about ourselves as readers. As with the initial sharing, I might choose the student to share based on our discussion during the class period, or I might ask who would like to share. As students share their thinking, I write down what they have to say in my smart book; later I type or write up their thinking and display it prominently so that all students can benefit.

I collect their sticky notes or handouts as they are leaving because each is tangible—and, yes, measurable—evidence of students' thinking that will be assessed with a rubric (see appendix B). There are probably as many ways to organize this evidence as there are teachers teaching. I use envelopes labeled with the homeroom teacher's name and today's date; after all, I will have from two to five more classes coming into the library that day.[2] Another teacher in our building uses folders for each student that are organized chronologically so that students can see their progress.

The structure described above remains the same for every session. Someone once asked me if students become bored doing the same thing each time. My response was an emphatic "No." Each book is a different adventure, a brand- and grand new world the student has self-selected based on his or her interests. In addition, the tools I have students use to record their thinking can and do vary. Sometimes I have students speak aloud their thinking to a tape recorder; students then use the tape to aid them in transferring their thoughts from their heads to their papers. At other times I might have students use word-processing software, or concept-mapping software like Inspiration, to help scaffold their thinking, reading, and writing. Students might convey their visualization through a drawing program like Kid Pix Deluxe.

By teaching how good readers read, we liberate our readers by providing access to the strategies they need to make meaning. And this truly is an act of liberation, as the statistics about who is reading what and where—the socioeconomic realities behind our circulation stats—reveal. In the succeeding chapters I describe why and how to teach each strategy in depth and for every age group because it *is* our business to provide the keys to the magic kingdom of reading to every reader who enters our doors.

NOTES

1. "Crisscross applesauce" because, with ankles crossed and folded under the body, children (and we must remember that these are real children with a full range of attention and behavioral challenges) are not able to kick/disturb nearby students, and with hands cupped like they are waiting to receive a bowl of applesauce, they are not fiddling with pencils, library books, or their neighbor's hair. We have already made the connection that it looks like we are ready to receive knowledge. It is for much this same reason that I use carpet squares as a management technique. Students put their library books under their squares so that they are not distracted during modeling time, but the books are readily available for guided, dependent, or independent practice. In addition, we have spent time at the beginning of the year talking about each square being that person's personal space, and we do not invade anyone's space without permission.

2. A brief reminder about maintaining your sanity. You cannot and indeed should not grade every single thought your students express. I generally grade the evidence immediately after introducing the strategy the first time (it is much easier to correct misconceptions if caught early) for one of the dependent practices (to see if students are ready to move on to independent application) and for one of the independent practices as a summative assessment. Depending upon the grading requirements of your school district, only one of these, the summative assessment, would actually make it into your grade book.

The Invitation

2

Creating a Community

The question of who reads is one of particular social importance. Reading is both a reflection of disparate education levels and a way of bridging the differences among them.

National Endowment
for the Arts,
Reading at Risk

*T*here is something sacred about the role of librarian, about our profession. We are, and always have been, keepers of the gate, guardians and guides to the ark of human knowledge. Entrance through our doors admits one to infinite worlds, magical kingdoms, and the treasure trove of knowledge created by our world's best thinkers, artists, and scientists. But the pool of those seeking entrance is shrinking, in part because of a national decline in reading comprehension scores.[1] On the 2003 National Assessment of Educational Progress, 38 percent of fourth graders and 28 percent of eighth graders could not demonstrate basic reading skills for their grade level (*Education Week*, Sept. 15, 2004). Equally disturbing are the findings from *Reading at Risk: A Survey of Literary Reading in America*, which show that literary reading is declining dramatically, with fewer than half of American adults reading literature (National Endowment for the Arts 2004). The trend is even more prevalent in poor, urban neighborhoods, as demonstrated by decreasing circulation rates;[2] data from the Facilities and Services Plan for Enoch Pratt Free Library show that materials circulation decreased by 32 percent between FY 1998 and FY 2002. In-house use of materials during the same period decreased by 33 percent. The correlation between poverty and low reading achievement is well documented. The

United Nations Committee on Human Rights and Poverty Reduction defined "being excluded from the world of reading and communication" as one of the three fundamental elements of human poverty (2004, 13).

Equally well researched is the link between passive readers and poor comprehension skills. Passive readers are not engaged in meaningful ways with the text. In addition, these less-than-proficient readers do not utilize comprehension strategies to increase either understanding or engagement. For libraries, both public and school, to increase their patron base, much must be done to transform passive readers into actively engaged members of a community of strategic readers and thinkers; however, the benefits of transforming our libraries into communities that nurture reading and thinking extend far beyond simply increasing our patron base.[3] What books, how, and to whom we choose to present them determine who enters the kingdom, and the consequences of our choices have serious economic ramifications. Of people with the lowest literacy skills, 43 percent live in poverty, and 70 percent of prison inmates read at the lowest proficiency levels (U. S. Department of Education 2000).

Yet it need not be this way. Books do transform lives by opening new vistas, as I well know. It was a blistering hot day in the summer of 1968 when books first opened the world to me; their pages showed me a place beyond poverty and fear, a place with unlimited horizons, possibilities, and ideas. I was twelve that summer and the world, as I knew it then, was encompassed by the fourteen row house–lined blocks of an area in southwest Baltimore City called Pigtown. The area had once housed hardworking German immigrants, like my grandparents, who drove pigs down the main street to the slaughterhouse, but poverty and drugs had transformed the neighborhood. Broken glass and needles glistened in the alleys, and rats played more frequently than children in the school yard of Charles Carroll Barrister Elementary. Fear was tangible; it stalked the streets and haunted one's dreams.

So too did hopelessness until the first assault of the War on Poverty arrived in the unlikely guise of a middle-aged, wiry-haired woman driving a Bookmobile. I think now how brave she was to approach what surely looked like a gang of hoodlums and thugs hanging out on a street corner in one of the toughest sections of the city with offers of free books. I distinctly remember one of my friends telling her, "Ain't nothing free," and her reply that "books are; learning is; and what's more is that there is enough power in books to change the world." We laughed and followed her in—mostly, I must admit, to see what the crazy lady would do next. What she did was show us row after row of brand-new books, each one containing a world filled with infinite marvels. Literature became my touchstone and books my wellspring of hope. I quickly developed into a voracious reader and knew that I wanted to share my hunger for learning with others—for the ability to read has been my salvation and my link to the best the world has to offer.

My story is not unique; one common denominator that links those who have escaped the bonds of poverty is the importance of books and libraries. People as diverse as Oprah Winfrey and Dr. Ben Carson, pediatric neurosurgeon at Johns Hopkins Hospital, acknowledge how books and libraries transformed their lives.[4] Oprah tells of how her father, Vernon Winfrey, saw to it that his daughter read a book and wrote a book report each week. Dr. Carson recounts when he first knew he was smarter than his grades in school would indicate. His mother, when she saw her son's failing grades, required him and his brother to read two library books a week and "to give her written reports even though, with her own poor education, she could barely read what they had written." As a result of his reading, Ben recognized rock samples his teacher had brought in for the class, and "It was at that moment that I realized I wasn't stupid," he recalled later. Both Winfrey and Carson acknowledge that they were forced to read. How do we reach readers without that parental support? How do we create a community where children are so actively engaged in reading that they would choose to read rather than go to recess or play yet another video game?

Former poet laureate Rita Dove would tell us that it begins with allowing students to self-select texts:

Going to the library was the one place we got to go without asking really for permission. And what was wonderful about that was the fact that they let us choose what we wanted to read for extra reading material. So it was a feeling of having a book be mine entirely, not because someone assigned it to me, but because I chose to read it. There was an anthology up there. One anthology of poetry. It was a purple with gold cover, I'll never forget. It's really thick. It went from Roman times all the way up to the 1950's at that point. And I began to browse. I mean, I really was like browsing. I read in it a little bit. If I liked a poem by one person, I would read the rest of them by that person. I was about eleven or twelve at this point. I had no idea who these people were. I had heard of Shakespeare, sure, but I didn't know the relative value of Shakespeare, of Emily Dickinson, or all these people that I was reading. And that's how my love affair, I think, with poetry began. This was entirely my world and I felt as if they were whispering directly to me.

My students would agree. Despite poverty rates that exceed 50 percent of the total student population and in spite of a lack of reading support and models at home, our students love to read; books of all kinds speak directly to them because they have learned how to engage in a dialogue with the text. They read regularly and for enjoyment at lunch, during recess, and, as a result of various reading incentive programs, at home. Visit Lansdowne Elementary's cafeteria on an average day and you will see students reading, discussing, and sharing favorite parts of their books. Listen to their conversations about books and you will think you have been transported to a much more affluent and literate community.

How do you transform apathetic readers into a community of engaged, strategic thinkers and readers? The first step is transforming the physical environment, including the lighting, how books are displayed, and the number and type of reading nooks and conversational areas. (See chapter 10 for other suggestions for arranging the physical spaces and ideas to implement strategy instruction in our libraries immediately.) Next you enhance how you help your patrons select books by modeling for them browsing, previewing, skimming, and selecting that "just right" book. Then you begin to create a community by fostering discourse about books during storytime, online, and in person through book clubs, blogs, and scaffolded dialogues. To counter possible parent objections and to involve them in the process of creating critical readers and thinkers, you create monthly newsletters or brochures to educate parents about the importance of not only reading books but also responding to books.[5] Finally, you resolve to share with your students the keys to unlocking the kingdom of reading: the comprehension strategies proficient readers use to become actively engaged in the most important task of all—making meaning of the world around us.

How to Model Browsing, Previewing, Skimming, and Selecting

Encouraging students to self-select texts does not stop with just that—encouragement. Students need to be taught how to self-select texts—books that will take them from here to there in their journey as readers. Dove's discovery of the poetry anthology that shaped her future does not have to happen serendipitously; in fact, if we want to reach all of our readers, we cannot rely on them accidentally stumbling upon that "just right" book. To engineer such discoveries, we must apply the same attention usually devoted to a reference interview to the task of helping readers select texts that will help them grow by modeling how to browse, preview, skim, and use guidelines for selecting fiction, nonfiction, poetry, plays, and periodicals.[6]

In my early years as a library media specialist, I devised numerous lessons for students on how to use the library's catalog. Students were taught how to search by author, title, subject, and keyword; they diligently practiced these search strategies, but never quite got around to checking out a book both because they lacked knowledge about which authors and titles to search for and because it took them too long to type in the information and conduct the search. Students who conducted subject or keyword searches were marginally more successful, but they still encountered difficulties when they went to the shelves to find their books both because alphabetical order involving more than one letter is difficult and because students do not even learn about decimals until the intermediate grades.[7] Finally, once the book was located, the reading level might be too high or low; the cover illustration not what they had pictured; or the book's physical dimensions disappointing, for example, a picture book for a child so proud of his reading abilities that he wants to check out only chapter books.

The majority of my students did not browse the shelves, and it wasn't until I began reading works by Pearson and Dole (1987) on the importance

Picking a just right book helps you go to harder books.
—MWJ

Pick a just right book because you will feel happy and you will learn to read.
—SOP

of modeling and articles by Vygotsky (1978) on proximal development that I began to understand what I perhaps should have known from the beginning: students cannot do that which they have never seen. Most of my students had never seen anyone browse shelves because 84 percent of our students had never been in a public library.[8] Before I begin modeling what browsing looks and sounds like, I read aloud the passage where Dove talks about discovering the poetry anthology that shaped her future, and I ask students to think about why selecting the right book is important.

After students share their responses, I tell them that the way most good readers find books is by browsing the shelves and conducting an internal dialogue about what they know about themselves as readers. Students follow me over to the shelves with their sticky notes so that they can record what browsing looks and sounds like. They observe as I browse and think aloud about how I select books.

I begin by tilting my head to the side so that I can more easily read the titles and talk about the things I look for in a title. For example, if the title contains the words *dragons, unicorns, mystery, castles,* or any of the topics I know I like reading about, then I'm going to stop and delve a little deeper. I model pulling the book from the shelf and using our guidelines for selecting "just right" books:

- The 5-finger rule[9]
- The Goldilocks strategy[10]
- Reading the summary on the back or flap of the book
- Taking a picture or book walk
- Skimming the first few pages
- Asking yourself questions like these:

  Have I read other books by the same author that I liked?

  What genre is this book?

  Is this a book in a series? If so, do I need to read the earlier titles to understand what is happening in this story?

  Do I have a personal connection to the book?

  Have any of my friends read the book? If so, do they recommend it?

I felt like the Pied Piper the first time I modeled effective browsing as I looked at the line of students with their heads tilted just so, wandering down the aisles for that book that whispers to them, "Try me." In later lessons I model for students how to look for books by genre, author, and Dewey classification. I also show them how to use online sites, like Book Adventure and Planet Book Club, to find books.[11]

Just as students need to be actively engaged in the process of comprehending what they are reading, so too must they be actively involved in the process of self-selecting a book to read. Too many children come to the library with a list of books their parents or teachers think they should read. Though many of these are excellent books, the child learns little about himself as a reader. Instead, he or she methodically and sometimes mechanically checks each book off and moves on to the next title on the list. Books are too important to be selected only through the use of lists; books can and do open new vistas, bridge economic differences, and provide the tools to help eradicate the plague of poverty. Helping readers select "just right" books is a solemn responsibility and one for which librarians are particularly well trained.

How to Foster Discourse about Reading

I remember before automation looking at the names of children who had signed out the book before me and wondering if they had the same feelings, the same sense of wonder and awe, as they read. I would speculate about their thoughts and question if their brains, like mine, had tingled, come alive with the infinite possibilities the author had presented. I would wonder if they had seen themselves, as had I, as the main character, or learned how to deal with bullies and loss as I had by reading the pages. I can even recall buying used books and looking for signs of intelligent life— the annotations, underlining, highlighting—that let me know that someone else had passed this way. And I think about what we lose when readers cannot have that intimate contact, that hands-on and minds-on engagement with a book, *and* the community of readers who have participated in that same experience. To create a community of readers in our libraries, we need to provide the models and the arenas for conversations to take place through the creation of book clubs, blogs, and scaffolded dialogues.

Tanya Auger (2003) summarizes current research about the benefits of participating in book clubs:

Tens of thousands of teachers and millions of students now take part in student-centered literature circles, also called book clubs or literature study groups, and the research on this phenomenon is on the rise (Daniels 2002). Studies have shown that when students are involved in authentic conversation about literature, they are more engaged in their reading (Alpert 1987; Enciso 1996), and they take more risks (Eeds and Wells 1989). During small-group discussions, students voice emotional responses to literature (King 2001). Literature circles also promote students' motivation to read and have been shown to improve students' reading levels and performance on tests (Davis, Resta, Davis, and Camacho 2001).

Book clubs can be formed either to study a particular curriculum connection or simply to discuss a certain book or strategy. Clubs may meet during lunch, after school, or—if the club is linked to the curriculum—during regularly scheduled library period. For some clubs, like the American Girl Club and our nonfiction club, I might have long waiting lists. In other cases, like the two students who wanted to form a club based on the Dragon Slayers' Academy book series, too few students may be interested to sustain a club, so I might show them how to join a virtual or online book club. A minimum of five students are needed to maintain lively discussions, and more than eleven students usually results in at least a few students sitting out during the conversations. As with adult book clubs, the most difficult decision is deciding which books to read and in which order to read them. For kids' book clubs, I recommend meeting once a week; any less than that and children begin to lose interest. Students already know what good conversations look and sound like from our discussions during their library class; the following statements are just a few of their suggestions:

"The best way to start a conversation is to share a question or a connection you have with the story."

"It's best to sit in a circle or at a round table so everyone can see one another."

"You do not raise your hand to share, but you do wait for a pause in the conversation."

"Don't retell the story; we've read it!"

"Use specific examples to support what you're saying."

"You always listen respectfully to what others are saying, even if you disagree."

"Different opinions make the conversation more interesting. If we all agree, it's going to be pretty boring!"

"There are no know-it-alls! We learn from each other."

Blogs are yet another way to encourage students' conversations about books and have the added benefit of encouraging students to write their responses. Other benefits are just as obvious: readers need not be at a specific place or available at a specific time to participate in a blog. In the act of creating their responses, either orally or in writing, students' thoughts coalesce, take form and meaning. Blog software is free and readily available. In addition, posting to the blog is quick and easy. Unlike chat rooms, I don't have to worry about pedophiles dropping into our blog; all conversations are posted and e-mail addresses, unlike screen names, are not part of the posting. Because students are publishing their thoughts to the Web, I do need to obtain parent permission, which is usually granted once I tell them that the blog is password protected. I also share with parents the benefits of creating an online community where students read, write, and think about books.

To scaffold students' dialogues, I have developed a number of forms to frame both their responses to what they are reading and to other readers.

I wondered as I was reading . . .

_____
_____
_____
_____.

Responses:

_____
_____
_____
_____
_____
_____
_____
_____
_____
_____
_____
_____
_____
_____
_____
_____
_____
_____
_____
_____
_____
_____
_____
_____
_____
_____
_____
_____
_____

Scaffolding, like modeling, is critically important for developing students' abilities; it provides the support or framework students need as they move toward increasingly more complex and independent use. Unlike other teacher-created forms, however, these forms remain in the book; their purpose is not only to structure students' responses but also to initiate an ongoing dialogue about the text.[12] The comment–response format encourages readers who may never meet in person to establish an ongoing dialogue about a personally significant book; it is like responding to threads in an online conversation. For example, students might choose to use the Question/Response form to ask questions as they read or respond to questions other readers have asked (see appendix B for other examples).

Sticky notes and index cards kept in the pockets are just a few other ways we can facilitate students' ongoing dialogue. When our conception of a library extends beyond the physical walls to the community we hope to create, librarians will create many other innovative and interactive means for continuing the conversations. Our mission, after all, is to promote "the creation, maintenance, and enhancement of a learning society" (ALA 2005), one where critical discourse is not limited to the elite, the few, but is open to and inclusive of all.

NOTES

1. Other widely cited causes are an increase in Internet use and a decrease in the amount of time available for recreational activities like reading.
2. Several researchers have argued that surveys that identify types and levels of use are a better indicator than circulation statistics of the vitality of a library branch in low-income neighborhoods (Koontz 2005).
3. "Surely," I can almost hear someone comment, "school libraries do not need to worry about a shrinking patron base. After all, the patron base of a school library is the population of the school." In an age of diminishing funds for education, school libraries that do not justify their existence by increasing engagement, comprehension, and test scores will surely feel the ax.
4. The following narratives from Carson, Winfrey, and Dove are taken from http://www.achievement.org.
5. Who, you might ask, would not want to join or want their child to enter this literate community? In tight-knit communities—whether they be built on economic conditions or religious and cultural affiliations—some people feel threatened, and justifiably so, by the power of the word. The fear is that by seeing other worlds the children will grow up to leave the communities that raised them. Some fear not only that the children will move away but also

Creating a Community

that the literature they read will teach them to denigrate their culture, community, and religion. People do not covet what they do not know exists, they argue, but books, like other media, conjure the riches of the world. In our outreach efforts we must make sure to validate all of the participants in our pluralistic society, and in our selection decisions we must make sure that the communities portrayed on our shelves are all-inclusive.

6. I have seen many forms and tutorials on how to conduct a reference interview; I have never come across one for the critically important task of helping a reader choose a "just right" book.

7. One day soon I hope the technology that already exists (and is used successfully by online bookstores) for building a reader profile, recommending titles based on titles previously chosen, and alerting the patron when new titles of interest to that reader arrive will be incorporated into our catalog software.

8. The number was derived from the number of students who did not have a public library card and confirmed by parent surveys.

9. To use the 5-finger rule, younger students close one hand into a fist as they begin to read the first page. Each time they encounter a word they do not know, they put up one finger. If by the end of the first page they have five fingers in the air, then that book is too hard for them. Students know to put that book back on the shelf and try it again later when they have become better readers. If by the end of the first page they have no fingers in the air, then that book may be too easy for them. They may want to select another book that will challenge them to become a better reader. Older readers follow the same process, but they only visualize the fist. As with all rules about book selection, there are exceptions. I have students who are fascinated by a topic, like dinosaurs. Because they are intrinsically motivated by the subject, they use subheadings, captions, illustrations, and other text features to access meaning from a book that might otherwise be too hard for them.

10. Students use the Goldilocks strategy before they apply any other book selection strategy. To use the Goldilocks strategy, students look at the spine of the book. They then ask themselves, "Is this book too small, too big, or just right for me?" The benefits of utilizing this strategy are obvious: students can quickly browse the shelves for that "just right" book, and it prevents, for example, first graders from checking out a six-hundred-page book just because they have seen the movie.

11. To investigate other resources, go to "Booktalk!" a research model I created to help students find books; it is available at http://www.bcps.org/offices/lis/models/bktalk/index.htm. Simply click on the "Bookfinder" button to see many more resources to help your students find great books.

12. I was initially concerned that students might write inappropriate comments on the forms, but my fears were allayed by the realization that nothing stops students from writing vulgar or derogatory comments in books as it is, yet I rarely have that problem.

3

Connecting

Books—stories—are things that draw us to them. They speak across the globe; they reach across frontiers. They bring together the imaginary and the real, the local and the universal, the present and the past. They bring us together, just as they did when the first stories were told by firelight in ancient caves. They bring us together because each of us has that thing that is both ordinary and quite astonishing: the imagination, which allows the writer and the reader, the teller and the listener to reach out to each other.

David Almond

onnecting is the first strategy I introduce because the ability to connect the text[1] to the reader's experiences is not only the first step toward reader engagement but also, and just as important, the first step toward realizing that we are not alone—that people who may look very different from us and who may have lived during a different time or in another place share our hopes, dreams, fears, and experiences. In addition, by identifying with the character and the problem the character is facing, the reader takes the first fledgling step toward developing empathy. The ability to make connections from one text to another forms the basis for author and genre studies as well as for analyses of literary movements and periods, like Romanticism. Finally, the ability to connect the text to events in the real world gives flesh to disembodied concepts like slavery, freedom, poverty, and war.

Still, the first time I introduce connecting strategy, I have to give myself a little mental shake, a "Hey listen up" pep talk. For years, storytime in my library was a production complete with different voices for different characters, props, and, yes, sometimes puppets. I rehearsed the telling of each tale and worked hard to improve its delivery. I chose songs or fingerplays, depending on the age of my audience, as a before-reading activity. A craft or activity related to the story always followed.

Before I read the story aloud, I did allow a limited dialogue about the book, seeking to activate students' prior knowledge and increase interest. For example, I would always ask:

Based on the title, what do you predict this book will be about?

Does the cover illustration confirm or contradict your prediction?

Who is the author, and what do we know about him or her?

Can we tell from the title, cover, or author what genre this book is?

But once storytime began, I expected all of my little friends to be an audience of good listeners. More than once, I now shamefacedly admit, I turned a baleful glance on any child who had the temerity to raise his or her hand while I was telling the story. And after the story, I would ask the standard comprehension questions:

What was your favorite part of the story?

What problem did the main character face, and how did he or she solve it?

What happened in the beginning, middle, and end of the story?

How did the setting contribute to the story?

After students answered my questions, storytime was officially over, and we never revisited or reread that book again.

I share this because I know that I am not the only librarian—school or public—to conduct storytime as a performance, albeit sometimes a marvelous one. Yes, I have seen children enthralled, their eyes lit with that special magic, but when storytime was over—when that last page was turned—their engagement with the text stopped, or perhaps never really began because they were not engaged by the story, but by my telling of it.

Ellen Fader (2003) notes:

Public libraries have been presenting fun and interactive storytimes for many years, engaging children and helping them love books and libraries. These programs typically include a combination of short and long books, music and action rhymes. Children are surrounded with stimulating speech and interesting topics, creating a language and literacy experience beneficial to children's development. These storytimes model for parents how to read enthusiastically and involve their children in books.

These stories do not, however, model for parents how to enhance their children's ability to eventually become independent strategic readers. Nor do they show children how to become active participants in the process of making meaning. Children are actively engaged in the songs, fingerplays, and craft activities but not in the most critical component: understanding the story. Storytime as it is currently practiced represents the traditional view of readers as empty vessels waiting passively to receive knowledge from an outside source.

Fader continues:

> Recent research in the field of emergent literacy has led to the development of new best practices for public libraries that want to help parents and teachers of preschool children get ready to read. Storytimes that incorporate these practices differ in subtle ways from the storytimes described above. [If we want our patrons to become actively engaged readers,] library staff will also demonstrate specific techniques that facilitate emergent literacy, since how adults read to preschoolers is as important as how frequently children listen to stories.

Simply telling a child a story does nothing to increase that child's ability to comprehend the written word independently, and children cannot love or come to value what they do not understand. Asking questions about the text also does little to increase students' comprehension. Proficient students, not readers, learn how to intuit what answer the adult is looking for and to provide it. Only teaching students how to use comprehension strategies through modeling, guided, dependent, and independent practice increases children's abilities to understand independently what they are reading.

Text-to-Self

As a result of my resolve to teach comprehension strategies, storytime in my library now looks very different. The first storytime of the year, whether to kindergarten or fifth-grade students, begins with me modeling how good readers connect the text to their experiences, to other texts, and to events in the world. I model what connecting looks and sounds like with a picture book by Jerdine Nolen, *In My Momma's Kitchen*. I use Nolen's book because of the many memories it evokes: everything good that ever happened in my life, every triumph—that 100 on a spelling test—was celebrated in my mama's kitchen. And every trouble was consoled, usually by chocolate chip cookies still warm from the oven.

Students have already gathered their sticky notes, pencils, and the "just right" books they will use later in the lesson. My little friends, students in kindergarten through second grade, have arranged their carpet squares in a circle and are seated crisscross applesauce with their supplies neatly tucked under their squares. My older friends, students in third through fifth grades, have gathered their chairs in a circle, and I gratefully pull up my chair (getting up from that crisscross applesauce position becomes more challenging as we get older).

I begin by telling students that today I'm going to model a strategy, connecting.[2] First I define connecting: Readers using what they know to understand what they read by relating the text to their personal experiences, their prior experiences with other texts, and their knowledge of world events and history. Because this is an elementary school, I provide visual cues to help my students remember the definition (see figure 3-1).

FIGURE 3-1

Connections Worksheet

Text-to-Self 	Text-to-Text 	Text-to-World 
• I act out stories too! • I get mad and sad like Grace does when someone tells me I can't do something. • Connecting helps me know what Grace will do because I know how she feels.	• Wendy and Grace both like adventure. • Oliver is called a sissy when he wants to dance. • Grace is told she can't be Peter Pan because she is a girl.	• The book makes me think that boys and girls should be able to do whatever they want. I also think that people who don't let you follow your dreams are mean.

Name: Brittany

Next I explain what research tells us about how good readers use the strategy. By connecting what happens in the text to their experiences, good readers know how the characters feel and will probably act. Proficient readers activate their schema or background knowledge about subjects, like dinosaurs or how to bake a cake, to help them understand what is happening in the text. Good readers use their experiences with other texts to help them comprehend. In addition, proficient readers use their knowledge of current events and history to provide a framework for understanding what is happening in the text.

Finally, I give students their job: as I am modeling the strategy, they should be observing what I do and say, so we can make a checklist of what connecting looks and sounds like. I begin, as I want them to, by looking for connections before I even open the book. "Wow," I say to the audience I pretend I can neither see nor hear, "I have a connection before I even open this book! Everything good that ever happened to me was celebrated in my mom's kitchen. I remember when I finally got a 100 on my 8 times tables how we danced around the kitchen. I wonder if they celebrate good things in her momma's kitchen. I'm going to record my connection so I don't lose track of it."[3] Then I take my pad of sticky notes, write T-S for a text-to-self connection in the top left-hand corner, and record my connection. I continue thinking aloud: "It's a tentative connection because I'm not sure that good things happen in her momma's kitchen, but I think based on my experiences that maybe good things will be celebrated there."

Next I look at the cover illustration, which depicts a little black girl in her momma's kitchen. Out loud I think about the differences: "We are both girls, but she is black and I am white. I wonder if that makes a difference. [I ignore the four or five hands that immediately shoot up in the air to answer my question.] I'll have to think about that as I read." I record my connection, we are both girls, on another sticky note that I have also coded T-S for text-to-self and place the sticky note on the cover, where I had that thought.

I pause and say, "Let me do a little self-check. Good readers always think about what they know that might help them understand the book even before they open it! I've done that. They also think about what they know about themselves as readers. I know that I like books where girls are the main character, because then I feel like I am in the story. I'm a little worried that our experiences might be different because she's black and I'm white, but I'll read on to see if that makes any difference."

After I read aloud and think aloud through the first few pages, I stop and ask students to share, not their connections just yet, but their observations about what connecting looks and sounds like. I record their observations on chart paper, guiding their responses by asking clarifying questions, and always praising their smart thinking. For example, when Zachary of the wildly waving hand says, "It made you think about your mom," I respond, "Wow, that's really good observing." To make his response more global, I might then ask, "So let me make sure I understand you: you're saying I connected what happened in the story to important people in my life, is that right?" After Zachary solemnly nods his head, I write on the chart paper: "Good readers connect the text to important people in their lives." By this time, ten hands are in the air. I call on Katie who adds, "It's not just the people. Good readers also connect the book to important places in their lives, like her mom's kitchen." Already the children have begun to use the framework I modeled for their responses. I add Katie's response to our checklist. I call on the next child, who wants to add to the checklist "Good readers connect what happens in the story to what happens to them"—and so our list grows.

Their observations serve as a scaffold for students to use as they employ the strategy for the first time. As I read aloud a few more pages, students record their connections on sticky notes. Later, as we share their connections, I place their sticky notes over the places in the text where the connections occurred. The act of attaching a note is a physical reminder that their thinking is linked to a specific event, character, setting, or fact in the text. It is a substitute for the annotations thoughtful readers record in the margins, but better because students can actually lift this thinking from the text, rearrange it, discard what has been answered, expand on tentative thoughts, and see patterns and connections. Another benefit is that they can use this technique on library books!

Next it's time for students to take out their library books and read with a buddy. I set the timer to make sure that we have time for reflective sharing, and the students begin. They might choose to partner read, but much more likely they chose one person to be the reader and the other to record the connections for both of them on sticky notes. As students read, I circulate throughout the room monitoring conversations and conferencing with different groups. I use this opportunity not only to monitor comprehension but also to invite students to share when I see really good thinking going on in their group. Some of this conferencing occurs as I check students' books in or out.

When the timer sounds, students return to our circle, and I invite them to share not just their connections but also how connecting helped them to become better readers. The first few times we share, I might prompt students by saying, "I saw some really good thinking going on in Nate and Nick's group. Would you mind sharing with us what you figured out?" Nick and Nate are just bursting with pride to share their really big thought. As I had walked past their table, I overheard them heatedly discussing if it mattered that the main character was a girl. They had concluded that, though they preferred reading books where a boy was the main character, it didn't really matter in *In My Momma's Kitchen*. When I asked them to explain why, they thought for a bit and then said, "It just wasn't girl stuff happening in the kitchen." I knew they were on the track of an important thought: our experiences as human beings unite us despite differences in gender, race, ethnicity, religion, and culture, so I prompted the two to keep thinking and to share with the whole group. As I walked over to the next group, I could not help smiling. For a third-grade boy to admit that he might have something in common with a girl was a major leap.

The next group was stuck on a word, *scholarship*. They had used the context clues to figure out that in some way it helped the girl in the story go to college, but that was as far as they could get using picture and context clues. They were debating which strategy to use: using a resource, like a dictionary, or reading on as I started to check books in and out. It would have been quite simple for me to stop and define the word for them, but while that would have solved their immediate problem, it would not have helped them become independent, strategic readers.

Nick and Nate need little prompting when it's time to share our connections and what we learned about ourselves as readers. As they share that *sometimes* (their emphasis, not mine) it doesn't matter if it's a girl or a boy, I see other students in our circle nod their heads. Before I even finish saying, "Let's see if we can make their idea even more global," Krystin's hand is in the air. "I know what you're going to say. It doesn't matter that you're white and she's black either. That's what I tried to tell you before, but you wouldn't call on me!" She's absolutely right; I had seen her hand raised while I was modeling, but as a result of having to wait, she had gathered the evidence from the story she needed to prove her insight. In a community where racism, if not omnipresent, is at least always a specter, my students benefit from lots of experiences demonstrating that our differences are truly only skin deep. With the group's help, I add their responses to our

Connecting

checklist: by connecting to the story, we learn how we are like people who look different from us.

In just this short introductory lesson, students have seen the strategy modeled by a good reader, used the strategy with guidance in a whole group, and practiced the strategy in dependent practice with a peer. In lessons over the next few weeks, students will have ample opportunities to observe refinements of the strategy and to participate in guided, dependent, and independent practice.

Text-to-Text

A few weeks have passed since I first introduced connecting. We have spent those weeks exploring how connecting to the characters, setting, and events helps us to become better readers with increasingly more complex picture books. Assessments of students' sticky note responses (see the Reading Checklist and Rating Scale in appendix B) show that students are able to employ the strategy independently before, during, and after reading. No subgroup of Lansdowne's target populations (minority, English for speakers of other languages, low socioeconomic status, special education) and indeed no child has been left behind. Students' ability to make connections to understand the world around them has been unleashed on the written word, and even my most reluctant readers are excitedly engaged in making connections between their lives and the text. When I think of the years I spent suppressing children's connections with a baleful glare for interrupting storytime or an acerbic comment to the child who persistently wanted to share what happened to him, I want to track down every child and offer my abject apologies. I did not truly understand, I want to say to them, the importance of connecting to increasing engagement and comprehension.

Students are now ready to begin connecting one text to another they have read previously. The ability to connect text-to-text is critical to their growth as readers, for it is key to identifying the author's craft, characteristics of genres, common themes in literature, and the elements that create literary movements. My first-grade patrons and I have just finished forging text-to-self connections with Tomie dePaola's *Oliver Button Is a Sissy*, the tale of little Oliver Button who keeps going each week to Ms. Leah's Dancing School for tap dance lessons even though "almost every day" the boys call him a sissy. As a result of connecting students' experiences to the events in the text, we have had wonderful discussions about the meaning of courage and the importance of following your dreams.

To model how good readers make text-to-text connections, I have chosen the thematically similar *Amazing Grace* by Mary Hoffman. Hoffman's picture book tells the tale of the truly amazing Grace, who longs to play Peter Pan in the school play but is told by her classmates that she cannot play the main role because she's a girl and she's black. I begin by telling students that today I'm going to model a strategy, text-to-text connecting, which good readers use to become even better readers. I define the strategy and again provide picture cues for my non-readers or fledgling readers. I explain that good readers use text-to-text connections as another kind of experience they can connect to, and then I tell them that I will be modeling how they can use the knowledge gained from that reading experience to help them understand a new text. Their job, as always when I am modeling, is to observe what I do and say so that we can make a checklist for students to use as they practice applying the strategy.

Before reading, I think aloud about the title, author, and cover illustration. "The title," I tell them, "reminds me of a song we sing at my church." Several students nod their heads in agreement. "I'm thinking about what the song is about and wondering if the book is about church or God. Let me write down my connection." On the sticky note I write, "reminds me of the song we sing in church," and code the note T-S for text-to-self connection. Already a few hands are in the air to tell me that we are working on a different strategy, but I shake my head and continue with my think-aloud.[4] "I have never read any books by Mary Hoffman, so I can't use author knowledge to help me. Hmmm, the cover illustration depicts a young black girl who is missing her two front teeth, but I can't tell if she's going to church. On the back, it looks like she's dancing and twirling around. We don't dance at my church, so now I'm a little confused. Maybe it's about church and they dance at her church, or maybe amazing grace means something else. I guess I'll need to read on to find out."

I read aloud the first page about the little girl named Grace "who loved stories. She didn't mind if they were read to her or told to her or made up in her own head. She didn't care if they were in books or movies or out of Nana's long memory. Grace just loved stories. . . . And sometimes while they were still going on, Grace would act them out." I stop at the end of the first page and record another text-to-self connection: I love stories just like Grace does and I love to act them out. I return to the book and read the next two pages aloud: "Grace went into battle as Joan of Arc . . . and wove a wicked web as Anansi the Spider."

"Wow," I think aloud, "I know both of those stories. I bet each story will help me understand Grace's character. Let me see . . . Joan of Arc was very brave and Anansi was very clever. Let me record that." I code the sticky note T-T and record my thoughts. I continue reading aloud and recording my text-to-text connections as the ever-adventurous Grace hides "inside the wooden horse at the gates of Troy" and becomes "Mowgli in the backyard jungle." I stop and think aloud, "Maybe I was wrong about the text-to-text connection with the song we sing in church. I'm going to put that on the side for now because I don't think that will help me understand this story."

I pause again after Grace's teacher announces that the class will perform the play *Peter Pan* and Grace is told by her friend Raj that she can't be Peter because she's a girl. "I'm having another kind of text-to-text connection. The author didn't mention this book, but what is happening to Grace reminds me of what happened to Oliver in that story we just read. They were both told they couldn't do something they really wanted to do. I wonder if she'll keep trying like Oliver did. I think she will because she likes acting like heroes, and heroes never give up. I'm going to write that down because I think that's a really important text-to-text connection." After I finish recording my thoughts, I stop and ask students to help me create a checklist of what text-to-text connecting looks and sounds like. After I record their responses, I ask them to think about how it might help us to become better readers:

"It helps you know the character."

"It helps you think about what might happen next."

"It helps you find books you like."

As I read the rest of the story aloud, students record their text-to-text connections. We share their connections and discuss the differences: Oliver does not win the talent show, but Grace does win the part of Peter Pan, which leads to an interesting discussion about what is more important— winning or following your dreams.

As students line up to leave, I return *Amazing Grace* to the shelf, but I know it won't stay there long. Students will want to check the book out again and again, and so will I as we continue to make meaning. Already I am thinking that maybe there is a link between the hymn and the book—

that maybe what was lost and now found is the talent of all the little girls like Grace who were told what they could not do or be because of their gender or the color of their skin.

Text-to-World

This lesson on text-to-world connections is taking place in the computer lab so that we can use fee-based databases to find information about a very real-world topic: money. It is a follow-up to the lesson on text-to-world connecting that I did last week with my second-grade students using Judith Viorst's *Alexander, Who Used to Be Rich Last Sunday*. We decided at the end of last week's discussion that we needed more background information about kids and money. I begin by telling students that when a story includes either a real-world problem or an event that really happened, good readers know that they might need to increase their schema, or background knowledge, through research. To scaffold their research, I created a template in Microsoft Word that I then saved to the school's server.[5]

We decide that our key search terms will be *kids* and *money*. We identify synonyms for both terms, coming up with *children* and *cash* using the thesaurus built into Microsoft Word. For this lesson, we use SIRS Discoverer because the Advanced Search feature appears at the top of the result page; if we have to change our search terms or refine our search strategies from full text to title to limit our results, it's as simple as scrolling to the top of the page. I show students how to select "easy" as the reading level, and I model sifting through the results to find that "just right" article. Students already know that the computer is just another tool for accessing text and that we use the same strategies to gather information.

Once I have identified which article I want to use, I demonstrate how to copy and paste the entire article, including the source information, into Word so that we can annotate the text using the Insert Comment feature. The Insert Comment feature, I tell them, is just like using sticky notes because we can place our connections next to the text, rearrange, add to, or delete our comments as we make meaning. Another benefit of using Word is that my students who need additional support can use the AutoSummarize feature to help them access information from long passages. I model how a good reader makes connections between the text and the real world; then students select an article and begin. As students work, I circulate throughout the lab solving a few technical issues (you can't see your comments because you clicked out of Page Layout view) and listening in on discussions. Brandon "thought that kid was pretty dumb when he traded money for a bus token, but it says right here that most kids don't understand how much money is worth." Others are shocked by how much things cost.

When we share, the first thing many students want to talk about is the title, *Alexander, Who Used to Be Rich Last Sunday*. Based on their research, they now understand that Alex wasn't rich at all and that many kids do not understand the meaning of money. Students were able to make connections between what they read and the real world; as an added benefit, students may be empowered by their new knowledge to make good choices about spending and saving money.

NOTES

1. *Text* refers to any of the myriad of materials a reader needs to comprehend, from menus to newspaper articles to picture books to textbooks.
2. Telling and showing must go hand in hand if we want students to not only do as we do but also know why they are doing it. For too long we have either told students what to do without showing them how or shown them what to do without telling or explaining the reasoning behind the actions.
3. The first thing they will ask you is, "Is that for real? Did that really happen to you?" and you must be able to look them right in the eye and answer emphatically, "Yes." If you make up your connections, then do not be surprised if your students do the same.
4. We have established hand signals for emergency-only bathroom breaks and trips to the nurse, so I need not worry that pretending I do not see their raised hands will result in any disasters.
5. I use a template I created in Microsoft Word and dropped into my folder on our school's server so that students don't have to take time typing in the heading and setting up the options for Comments and Page Layout view. To set up the template (I use Word 2003; your menus may be slightly different), under the Tools menu, select Options. Click on the Track Changes tab. Check Use balloons in print and Web layout and Show lines connecting to text. Type in Search Terms; Synonyms; and Source. Save as a template to your server.

4

Visualizing

*Lead makes the words, images,
idle thoughts (doodles), specific
information—crucial and otherwise—
visible. . . . With the lead from a pencil
I can make thin delicate words and lines,
bold solid black forms, and wispy, smooth
gray shadings. All with the same soft lead.
Everybody can, anybody—no experience
necessary. Everybody can do it, from the
very beginning, right out of the box.*

Donald Crews,
"Ticonderoga #2"

When my children were little, we spent many happy hours cuddling and reading until, inevitably, they would have to get down so that I could wash clothes, do dishes, or wipe away the one thousand and one fingerprints that had appeared magically on every available surface. While I worked, they would draw pictures of the stories we just read and then track me down to present me with their pictures, usually when my arms were full of laundry or my hands soaked by dirty dishwater. I would immediately respond, "Wow honey, that's really wonderful. I love your use of colors. Hang that on the refrigerator so everyone can see your work." Never once would I ask them questions about their drawings, because I did not want to hurt their feelings by revealing that I had no clues what their drawings were meant to represent.

Now I know how revealing and important children's drawings are; their sketches reveal both their comprehension of and engagement with text. Research shows that proficient readers make meaning by creating their own set of unique mental images to accompany the text; poor or reluctant readers, on the other hand, have more difficulty visualizing and as a result became frustrated and disengaged with the text (Beers 2002). As Zimmermann and Hutchins (2003, 20) note, "When sensory images form in a child's mind as he reads, it is an ongoing creative act. Pictures, smells, tastes, and feelings burst forth and his mind organizes them to help the story make sense. It is this ongoing creation of sensory images that keeps children hooked on fiction, poetry, and much nonfiction."

Visualizing, "the innate ability humans have for bringing texts alive in their 'mind's eye' through mental pictures," is much more than an artistic response—although that in itself is something to be valued, nurtured, and cultivated (McPherson 2004). It is in the act of framing a response— artistic, oral, and written—that meaning takes shape and form, coalesces, and emerges as a synthesis of the interaction between reader and text. By valuing only the analytical response, either written or oral, we denigrate not only art but also a mode of expression that has communicated ideas or experiences since our earliest ancestors first drew on cave walls.

Critically examining their communication, what they have drawn or sketched, reveals much about what children did or did not understand as they read. If the sketch is rich in accurate details faithfully conveyed—even if the information is not quite artistically portrayed—then the reader was engaged with and understood the text. If significant details are lacking or inaccurately depicted, then there are gaps in the reader's understanding. Furthermore, details students do not remember to include in their visualization are details they are unlikely to recall as they make meaning or answer test questions. Having students explain or label their visualization helps reveal these gaps and serves as a valuable assessment tool. In addition, asking students to explain their visualization helps them summarize the text and in the process determine important ideas.

The benefits of visualizing are obviously not limited to its use as an assessment tool. Students who visualize what they have read or heard read aloud encode information from the story in both verbal and nonverbal formats; research by Paivio (1971, 1986; Clark and Paivio 1991) and Rieber (1994) clearly shows the advantages of processing information through dual modalities. Paivio, who developed the dual coding theory to provide a cognitive framework to explain the relationship between imagery and verbal processes, states that "human cognition is unique in that it has become specialized for dealing simultaneously with language and with nonverbal objects and events" (1986, 53). He posits that memory consists of two separate but related codes for processing information—one verbal and the other visual. The verbal and visual systems can work independently, but there are connections between the two systems that allow dual coding of information. When both systems are activated to process information, retention and recall increase. In study after study, Sadoski found that processing information verbally and visually resulted in greater recall and retention; he notes, "The mental imagery that we experience while reading, either spontaneously or induced by instruction, is now known to have powerful effects on comprehension, memory, and appreciation for text" (1999).

Modeling Visualizing

I introduce visualizing to my second graders by telling them that "today, I'm going to introduce a strategy that is absolutely 100 percent guaranteed to help each and every one of you get better grades on your next reading test." Immediately, students are interested; every elementary student I have ever taught wants to do well on tests. In fact, tests are a frequent and significant source of stress for children. I then define visualizing as a strategy used by proficient readers to create vivid mental pictures as they read. "For some readers," I tell them, "the images are so vivid and continuous that it is like they are creating a movie in their minds." In kid-friendly language I share the results of research that demonstrates how and why visualizing will help them retain and recall information from any text they read. Then I tell them that "we're going to test my theory that visualizing will help each one of you do better on tests by taking a reading quiz on *Lions at Lunchtime*," a Magic TreeHouse book by Mary Pope Osborne my second graders are reading. As is true of the other books I choose for modeling, only one of the reasons I chose Osborne's book is related to its suitability for strategy instruction. Other reasons for selecting *Lions at Lunchtime* are that it helps students achieve the science indicators for habitat, predator/prey relationships, and classification of animals as well as the language arts indicators for cause and effect, characterization, and plot development. It also introduces students to a wonderful series.

I model visualizing by reading aloud from the first two chapters. As I read aloud, I pause periodically to close my eyes and think aloud about the vivid images the words form in my mind. When Jack peers out of the window and through the leaves of the tree where the tree house landed, I too can see a giraffe with a sweet, goofy face eating the leaves, and I can feel its warm breath as it sniffs curiously at me. I can even taste the sweet, salty peanutty taste of the peanut butter Jack lugs around in his book bag. "It's even better than an illustration or even a movie because I can imagine what I would hear, smell, taste, touch, as well as see," I comment to my attentive audience. When Jack sees a huge grassy plain, a wide river, and *tons* of birds and animals, I stop and think aloud: "I'm having a little trouble visualizing this part because there are so many vivid details. To help organize my thinking, I think I'll sketch what I am picturing in my mind." I close my eyes so students can see me thinking and then begin to sketch Jack and Annie on the Serengeti Plain. I use Osborne's vivid descriptions to draw where the hyenas are in relationship to Annie and Jack. Then I add the other animals, sometimes making a guess about what a creature looks like. When I finish drawing, I comment, "Though it doesn't look much like the vivid picture I have in my mind, it does help me clarify what I am imagining because it helps me see how close Annie and Jack are to all of the animals.[1] It also makes me wonder why the other animals aren't running away. Aren't hyenas predators?" I ask.

Drawing or sketching the vivid mental images formed while reading is not, of course, necessary. After all, proficient readers form mental images all the time as they are reading without once sketching the images. Drawing or sketching their images does, however, help less proficient and fledgling readers develop and hone their use of this critically important strategy. In addition and as mentioned above, their sketches and the accompanying explanations serve as a quick assessment tool. Kindergarteners and first graders, at least for the first half of the year, orally explain their visualizations. Students in second grade and above write captions to explain their sketches.

After I finish modeling, students help me create a checklist of what visualizing looks and sounds like:

"You close your eyes and really think about the picture
   you're drawing in your mind."

"Yeah, your face gets all wrinkly, like when you're thinking
   really hard."

"Sometimes, you draw the picture in your mind. Sometimes,
   you draw it on paper."

"You talk about the picture."

"You explain the things the picture can't show, like what
   you hear, taste, and smell."

"You include lots of details."

"The drawing doesn't have to be perfect."

I read aloud the second chapter and guide students as they practice using visualization. Before I move on to the next two stages, I give students a reading quiz to demonstrate the benefits of visualizing as a test preparation. Students answer five multiple-choice or selected-response questions and write a Brief Constructed Response, a short essay that assesses students' comprehension of factual knowledge gleaned from the text on a standard 3-2-1 rubric. As I predicted, every student received a score higher than their average score.

What I did not predict, but what continues to surprise me, is how effective visualization is in increasing test scores. Not one student failed the reading quiz. In our target populations (low socioeconomic status and minority students) the increases are impressive: from a 42 percent passing rate (cutoff score of 70 percent) to 100 percent of students passing. Just as dramatic are the increases among students with ADHD and ADD. Whether the increases are due to dual coding or to the demands of multitasking (listening, visualizing, and sketching) would make for a fascinating and much needed research study.[2]

After the quiz, students select books about animals and habitats to use as they practice visualizing with a partner and independently.

Visualizing with Picture Books

Today I'm modeling point of view and how it limits what you can and cannot see with Chris Van Allsburg's tale of *Two Bad Ants* who decide to remain behind in the strange world they discover while searching for more of the beautiful sparkling crystals the queen ant loves to eat. Both the text and the illustrations are perfect for teaching visualization and point of view. The point of view of the two bad ants is limited by both their diminutive size and their lack of schema about the strange, new world. Van Allsburg's illustrations perfectly convey their limited point of view. At one point the illustration shows the ants flailing helplessly in a boiling black lake, or so it seems from their point of view. Another illustration reveals them clinging precariously to the face of a mountain, which actually is the exterior wall of the kitchen they soon invade.

Why visualize a text already replete with illustrations from a master illustrator? Simply viewing the illustrations might not lead students to the correct identification of the sparkling crystal as sugar, or of the boiling black lake as coffee. Only by visualizing the story and examining the illustrations were students able to pinpoint the setting of the strange world the two bad ants abandon their nest for when they finally decide, "Why go back?" when we can stay behind and eat these sparkling treasures forever. The other, "good" ants had quickly scurried back to the colony with their treasure for the queen because there was something about this strange world—where the "smells they had known all their lives, smells of dirt and grass and rotting plants, had vanished"—that made them nervous. Visualizing the story allowed students to see how point of view limits what the characters and, by extension, the reader, can and cannot see.

In a study of 120 fourth graders, Gambrell and Jawitz found that

> children in the group instructed to form mental images of their own as well as attend to illustrations significantly outperformed all the other groups on several measures of comprehension and recall. The imagery-only group outperformed the illustrations-only group on recall of story structure elements and complete recall of the story. (1993)

Students who did not see a single illustration, but who visualized the story as they read, remembered more of the story and were able to use the information to make meaning. Students who both visualized and viewed the illustrations scored higher on subsequent comprehension tests.

Visualizing with Nonfiction

Visualizing is just as effective with nonfiction or informational texts as it is with fiction. In the spring of every year, I gather my kindergarteners, a blanket, and Arthur Dorros's *Ant Cities* and head outside to the baseball diamond next to our school. We spread our blanket atop the pitcher's mound, which not so coincidentally is also the entrance to an ant colony; the elevation of the mound helps to prevent flooding in the chambers below. It is one thing for children to see an illustration of the interior of an ant colony in a book; it is quite another to visualize the ant colony under the ground where their feet tread every day. Visualizing helps students make that real-world connection and see the real-world application of discrete, sometimes boring, science facts.

Even though we are outside, students have their clipboards and pencils just like scientists in the field. We begin with students seated on the blanket's perimeter facing in, both to build a feeling of community and to diminish distractions, like the man walking his dog. In a previous lesson, I modeled for students how nonfiction helps us become better readers, so today students are ready for guided practice. On the top third of their paper, I encourage students to sketch the world around them. Most include our school and all draw us gathered on the blanket atop the pitcher's mound. As I begin to read aloud, students add the "miles of tunnels and hundreds of rooms" that lie just under our feet. I pause frequently and share what I am visualizing to provide guidance. I ask, "Can you picture in your head what's happening in the story?" or "What sounds do you hear? What details do you see? What colors? What smells? What tastes? What textures do you feel?" I also check their drawings to look for discrepancies that might indicate misunderstandings.

In addition, we stop frequently to compare the artist's conception with what we are imagining *and* observing. Students' renderings of the ant colony differ in several significant ways from the illustrator's. For example, students add several entrance tunnels because they observe ants entering and exiting from more than one hole. Later we will explore whether these are entrances to the same colony, as it would appear from how closely grouped the tunnels are, or if there is, as Dorros portrays, only one main entrance.

As students become more adept at visualizing the world beneath our feet, I gradually diminish the amount of guidance I provide. Students continue to sketch the activities Dorros describes occurring in each chamber as I continue to read aloud. Some excitedly flip to the back of their paper to enlarge certain chambers to show more detail. One student illustrates a connection; she draws her cat licking her kittens clean the same way worker ants lick the larvae clean. Others wonder if the pupae are indeed white as Dorros's illustrations suggest. They had depicted the pupae as smaller versions of the adult ant because they have seen tiny ants, which they assumed were baby ants. We conclude that we will have to do more research to see who is right.

As we pack up to go back inside, students are excitedly talking about creating visualizations of the ant colonies that must exist everywhere ants have been found, even "at the tops of the highest buildings and on ships at sea." Boring facts, like the worker ant carries the seeds to the colony, have taken life and meaning as students picture the tiny ant crawling through miles of dirt tunnels to reach the food storage chamber. By visualizing, my kindergarteners have been transformed into budding scientists intent on conducting additional observations and research.

Visualizing with Poetry

"Poetry," I tell my fourth-grade students, "is the perfect medium for visualization because poetry is imagery captured by the power of words. Great poetry always seeks to escape its captivity, threatening to spill over, burst forth and take shape and form." To help students remember and recall this, I have them close their eyes and visualize images sprouting in the white spaces between letters and growing until the lines of the letters are stretched to the breaking point trying to contain them.

Another benefit of using poetry is that the shorter selections allow students more time in each phase of instruction: modeling and guided, dependent, and independent practice. Each phase is equally crucial to the development of independent, engaged, strategic readers. The biggest mistake that teachers, including library media specialists, make when beginning strategy instruction is to subvert modeling into another teacher-centered discussion of the text. We do this with the best intentions in the world; we want our students to comprehend and treasure literature. However, if the modeling session takes thirty-five minutes of a fifty-minute period, then I am not modeling what I want students to do because I have left them insufficient time to put into practice the strategy they have seen modeled. If strategy instruction is to be successful and if students are to replicate independently the strategy they have seen modeled, then equal weight and time must be given to each stage.

In the first ten minutes of the period I model visualizing with a free-verse poem, "Tree Dancers," by Avis Harley. Students listen and take notes as I define free verse and talk about the how and why of its development. Then students observe and take notes as I visualize by sketching the lines: "Winds / sweeping over pines / shape limbs into / rigid images: / tree dancers / locked / in frozen rhythm— / silent tango partners."[3]

We talk about how the use of free verse, especially the placement of line breaks, helps to create the imagery. Then we take about five minutes to share how and why the author's diction, or word choices, creates vivid visualizations. In this lesson, instead of writing students' insights onto a chart or having them attach their sticky notes for me to rewrite later, I record their comments using the Rapid Fire feature of Inspiration, a concept-mapping software program (figure 4-1). The benefits of using Inspiration are many. First, it saves time, since I do not need to recopy the information. Second, we can easily group and reorganize ideas by simply dragging. Third, I can easily print copies of our checklist for students to use as they work with a partner in the three remaining stages of strategy instruction: guided, dependent, and independent practice.

I guide students as they visualize another poem from Harley's work and then conference with groups as students work with partners to visualize a third poem. Next, each student self-selects a book of poetry from the library's ample collection. Their mission is to find a poem that lends itself to visualization, sketch their visualization, and identify how the form of the poem (free verse, shape, or rhyme) affects its meaning.

Several of the fourth-grade girls choose poems from *Hoop Queens*, by Charles R. Smith Jr. Their favorite is about five-foot, eleven-inch WNBA superstar Ticha Penicheiro, who is "The Chef," serving "dishes with flair, / feeding teammates while twisting midair." Yet another benefit of using poetry to teach visualizing is that the poet's word choices help to build students' vocabulary. One student chose to type "The Chef" into Microsoft Word so that she could right-click on unfamiliar words and easily obtain a synonym. Of the five proven methods of vocabulary instruction, she was employing two: implicit and association methods. In implicit vocabulary instruction, students expand their vocabulary by reading a variety of rich text and being exposed to new words in context. In the association method of vocabulary instruction, students expand their vocabulary by "associating the familiar with the unknown" (NICHD 2000). Both methods, research

FIGURE 4-1

Poetry Concept Map

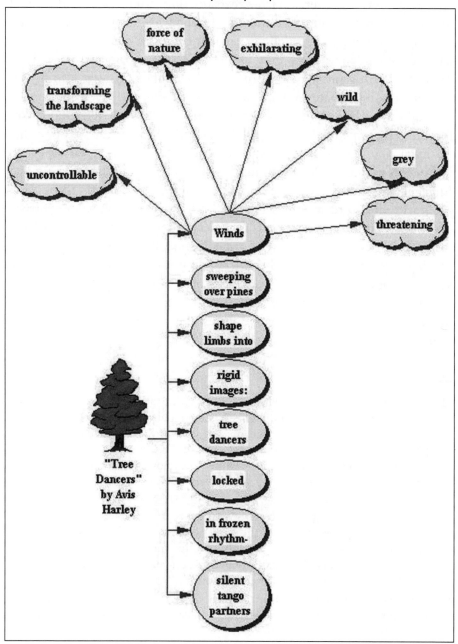

shows, effectively build vocabulary. While she was in Word, this student used the Scribble tool (in AutoShapes/Lines) to draw her visualization.

Mental images generated from texts not only can be expressed through drawings, sketches, paintings, and other graphic art forms but also can and should include dramatic retellings, enactments, and concept mapping. In later lessons in the poetry unit, students use visualizing to dramatically retell or enact narrative poems. In Cornelia Funke's *Inkheart*, Mo has the gift of bringing whatever he reads aloud to life; "My voice," he says, "brought them [the characters] slipping out of their story like a bookmark forgotten by some reader between the pages." Mo's gift can be ours when we learn how to visualize—see, taste, touch, hear, and smell—the text. Characters spring to life and strange worlds become intimate and familiar. Engagement, comprehension, and recall increase. And art will be fused again with literature and the sciences. But first we must show our patrons, many of whom do not develop this critical process independently, how to make the text come alive by creating mental images of what they are reading or we are reading to them. If we do not—"if children fail to create sensory images while reading, they suffer a type of sensory deprivation. . . . It would be like walking into a theater, sitting in a seat, and having the lights go down and nothing come up on the screen" (Zimmermann and Hutchins 2003, 20).

NOTES

1. My students know that drawing is not exactly my strength, but my drawing deficiencies encourage them. Unlike many models created by teachers, which are so far above what students can attain, my sketches could easily be produced by the least able of my students. As I tell them all the time, it's not the artistic rendering or composition that is important; it's representing the vivid mental image that formed as you were reading.

2. Increases in test scores among students with ADD and ADHD, though noticeable, are not as pronounced when students are simply asked to visualize in their minds; however, when the same population is asked to sketch their visualization, test scores increase dramatically. Anecdotal evidence from parents supports claims of increased concentration and focus while drawing or sketching in children with attention disorders.

3. Copyright © 2000 by Avis Harley, from *Fly with Poetry: An ABC of Poetry*, written and illustrated by Avis Harley. Published by Wordsong, Boyds Mills Press, Inc. Reprinted by permission.

5
Questioning

My mother made me a scientist
without ever intending to. Every
other Jewish mother in Brooklyn
would ask her child after school:
So? Did you learn anything today?
But not my mother. "Izzy," she would
say, "did you ask a good question today?"
That difference—asking good
questions—made me become a scientist.

Isidor Isaac Rabi,
"Great Minds Start with Questions"

*E*ven before I introduce questioning as a strategy, I can look out at my audience and pick the students for whom questioning will become their favorite strategy: my logical and analytical thinkers—those children filled to the brim with whys—our future scientists, engineers, philosophers, mechanics, and computer analysts. But first I know that with students in second grade and above I need to overcome resistance. My better readers will be hesitant to reveal their questions; they think they are supposed to have all of the answers. My below-grade-level readers wouldn't be caught dead asking questions, because they are very much afraid it will open them up to ridicule. Building a community of readers and thinkers must begin by dispelling the myth that good readers have all the answers; the reality, I tell them, is just the opposite: good readers have all the questions.

Research on proficient readers shows that good readers ask questions before, during, and long after reading. Decades of research clearly demonstrate the link between students' abilities to generate questions and increases in comprehension. Teaching children to ask questions as they read, the National Reading Panel reveals, results in independent, active readers. "By generating and trying to answer them [questions], the reader processes the text more actively" (NICHD 2000); as a result, comprehension increases.

Children need to be shown how good readers question the text as they are reading, and who better to show them than librarians? Very few professions know more about the art of questioning than librarians.

The scientific evidence for the efficacy of asking questions in comprehension was so strong that the panel recommended explicit instruction in self-questioning. The panel also suggested that question generation is best used as a part of a multiple-strategy instruction program. Despite the body of research supporting the benefits of student-generated questions, the paucity of student-generated questions Dillon (1988) noted more than a decade ago continues in classrooms today (Nist and Simpson 2000; Pressley 2000). Students spend far more time answering the generic "5 Ws and an H" questions than they do trying to understand what they are reading: *When* do the events happen? *Where* does the story take place? *Who* is the story about? *What* is the problem? *Why* did this happen? *How* is the problem solved?

Children can, and frequently do, answer the 5 Ws and an H, but *without* comprehending the text.[1] The complex themes, multifaceted characters, and author's rich, evocative use of language elude these lower-level questions, for these are the tools of a journalist, not of a student of literature. Children's literature is just that—literature—and literature that is worthy of the same degree of homage, scrutiny, and analysis we pay to its adult counterpart. The questions we need to model for students are those that arise naturally as a result of the reader's interactions with the text before, during, and after reading.

Modeling Questioning

The first time I introduce the strategy of questioning, I draw a question mark on a sticky note and ask students if they know what that symbol means. "It's a question mark," someone will reply. With some more prodding, students might add that you put it at the end of a sentence when you ask about something you don't know. Then I turn the sticky note upside down and ask students what the figure looks like now. Every child who has ever been fishing immediately raises a hand. "It's a fish hook, Ms. Grimes!" they shout out enthusiastically. "Who is on their bottom, crisscross, and can tell me what it is used for?" I ask. At least fifteen of my little ones sit back down, remember our rules for civilized conversation, and raise their hands. I call on the one, and there is always at least one, who reads well below grade level but who has a wealth of personal experience he or she is not able to connect to school. "It's used to catch fish," he or she proudly explains. "Can you tell us how it works?" I ask. A somewhat technical explanation ensues, which I usually restate as "So, the fish bites the hook, then you pull it up. Is that right?" (My experiences with fishing have never been this simple or successful, so one day, a little closer to retirement, I'm going to ask a few more questions.) "So let me make sure I understand this—the fish is caught or stuck on the hook?" I ask. As students nod their heads, I flip the sticky note and say, "Wow! Questions act just like fish hooks except instead of catching fish, good readers use questions to catch answers, but you already knew that, didn't you? That's why we read the questions first when we are taking a test." Students nod their heads solemnly. They already know what smart thinking it is to read the questions first when taking a test; it is in fact the first test-taking strategy we teach them.

"Now imagine," I tell them, "how much better if you are the one asking the questions! I'm going to model how good readers ask questions with *The Case of the Marshmallow Monster*, by James Preller." *The Case of the Marshmallow Monster* is the eleventh in a series of books about Jigsaw Jones, an overworked and underpaid detective who also happens to be in second grade. He's always on a case, so he is quite excited when he goes on a camping trip— that is, until Mr. Hitchcock tells the tale of the Marshmallow Monster, a creature no one has seen, or at least lived to tell about it! And then a bag of marshmallows disappears—and the chase for the culprit ensues.

I chose Preller's book to introduce questioning to this second-grade audience for four reasons, only one of them related to the text's suitability for generating questions:

1. It's October, so my patrons expect a good, scary story.

2. It's time to nudge my second graders into reading early chapter books.

3. Questions hook answers; series hook readers. Every good reader who has ever entered the doors of my library was hooked first by a series.

4. Mysteries naturally lend themselves to asking and answering questions.

I remind my students that good readers start thinking about the book before they read the first page. "For example, I had my first question when I read the title. Why marshmallow?" I wonder aloud as my students carefully observe what questioning looks and sounds like. "Is it a monster made out of marshmallows? If so, that doesn't sound very scary. When I think of marshmallows, I think of camping. I wonder if they meet a monster while camping. I better write my question down so I can keep track of it." Seamlessly, I connect, question, and predict. Even when a specific strategy is being modeled, students should never receive the impression that strategies are used in isolation. I code a sticky note with a question mark in the upper left corner and write "Why marshmallow?" Then I place it over the title. "Wow," I say aloud, "putting the sticky note on the title makes me think of another question I have about the title: Why case? I wonder if this is a detective story." I put a second sticky note over the title.

Students observe as I look at the author's name and listen as I explain that I have not read any other books by this author, so I have no background information to help me. Next I examine the cover illustration. "There's a puzzle piece on the front cover and written inside it says, Jigsaw Jones Mystery. I wonder if Jigsaw Jones is the detective. If so, is he really named Jigsaw? The word jigsaw reminds me of something, but I can't remember what. I'll have to keep thinking about that.[2] "Why Jigsaw?" I write on the sticky note and place it over the puzzle piece.

"Let me do a self-check. Good readers ask themselves questions before they read; I've done that. Good readers always think about what they know about themselves as readers. I know that I like to find answers to questions; that's why I became a librarian! If this is a detective story, I should be able to ask many good questions, but I may not find the answers until the end, so I'll have to remember to be patient and keep thinking about my questions."

I read the first chapter aloud, pausing to ask more questions and to reflect on the answers that leap out at me as a result of the questions I asked earlier. Simple questions like "I wonder where Jigsaw's mother is?" are immediately answered by the end of the chapter. Other questions, like "I wonder how missing marshmallows are related to a lake monster?" must wait until the end of the book for answers. Still other questions, like "I wonder if there are really such things as lake monsters?" might still leave us wondering long after we finish the book and propel us to read other books on the subject. I model writing just the key words from the question. For example, for the previous question I would write only "Are there monsters?"

There are two benefits to jotting down only the key words. Writing is still a labor-intensive activity for second graders; the less time they spend writing, the more time they can spend thinking. The second benefit is that students have additional practice identifying key words and ideas.

I stop at the end of the chapter and ask students to share their observations about what questioning looks and sounds like. Several children noticed that I asked questions before I started reading, so I add that first on the chart. Several then chime in that I asked questions while I was reading, so that too is added. As students respond, the list grows:

"Wrote just key words on the sticky note."

"Started questions with why."

"Wondered about the question."

"Connected questions to what you knew."

"Didn't ask yes/no questions."

"Kept reading even though you had a lot of questions."

Students take their sticky notes and pencils from under their carpet squares and listen as I explain that their job is to ask some really good questions as I read the second chapter aloud. They know that they do not need to wait for me to stop to begin writing down their questions; questioning, like connecting, should occur as part of the ongoing interaction with the text, not as an interruption. Learning how to maintain an internal dialogue while reading is important for developing comprehension (Buehl 2001). All

Good questions help me think about the book.

Asking questions is like me talking to the author.

the same, during the guided practice portion of the lesson, I pause periodically to give students a chance to think about the text. As students are thinking and writing down their questions, I peek over their shoulders to see who needs help and who has a great question to share. If I see a student struggling, I make a note to conference with that student first when students move to the next stage: dependent practice.

I read aloud the second chapter where the intrepid Jigsaw first hears the story of the Marshmallow Monster. One particularly voracious questioner, Alex, has to borrow my stapler to secure all of her questions. Every student has at least one question: "Is there really a monster?" It is a yes/no question but one whose answer is critical to the story, so we modify our checklist. Then I ask students to reflect on how asking questions helps them to become better readers.

Over the next few weeks, I continue to read aloud *The Case of the Marshmallow Monster* as students hone their abilities to ask questions and discover what to do when the answers do not leap out of the text.

Questions: Stepping Stones on the Path of Wonder

"Not only do questions help you become a better reader," I tell my students, "but also questions are the stepping stones to the path of wonder. You never know where a good question is going to take you, but you can be sure it will be an interesting journey." To encourage students' natural curiosity, I have them record all of the things they wonder about on an "I Wonder . . ." log (see figure 5-1). Students complete the first column as they read.

In another lesson, I model for students how to research their questions on the Internet or in books; however, students are never required to answer every question on their "I Wonder . . ." logs because I do not want to discourage their curiosity; rather, I hope to nurture it. For the same reason, I rarely grade or reward students for their research. I find that simply encouraging students' innate curiosity by allowing them to share what they discover is usually enough motivation; we need to allow students to experience that discovering information is intrinsically rewarding. By completing the "I found the answer in . . ." column, students begin to see a pattern of resources to use for which questions; in addition, they can use the third column to discover information about themselves as readers and researchers.

FIGURE 5-1

"I Wonder" Log

I wonder . . .	I discovered . . .	I found the answer in . . .
• What's the highest temperature ever recorded?	134° in California in 1913.	World Almanac for 2004
• At what temperature will animals start to die?		
• If and how do high temperatures cause thunderstorms?	when the high temperatures mix with cold fronts.	Eyewitness books Weather

Name: _Brandon W._

After students have had the opportunity to research several of their questions, we examine which resources students prefer to use. Then I ask them to think about why and how the resource helps them to become better thinkers and readers. For example, Sean prefers to use the online version of *New Book of Knowledge* because he thinks "encyclopedias are the best place to start your research because it gives you general background information." He likes the online version because, if there is a word he doesn't know, he only has to double-click it and then click on the Dictionary link to find the definition. He also likes that related news articles and a list of books for further reading are just a click away.

Harvey and Goudvis (2000, 86) describe another technique for encouraging questions. The students in Mary Urtz's fourth-grade classroom keep Wonder Books to record "questions on topics of interest, questions from their reading, and questions for research." Some students simply list all of their questions; others choose to use a two-column format to record answers. Miller's students (2002, 134) each had "a Wonder Box—a 3-by-5 file box they've decorated with small stick-on ladybugs, dinosaurs, birds, and flowers and filled with a stack of brightly colored index cards—'Wonder Cards'—on which to record their questions." Whichever method you choose to encourage your patrons' curiosity, know that by fostering questioning you are helping them to become critical thinkers, readers, and researchers.

Using Questions to Create a Community of Readers and Thinkers

One way to create a community of readers and thinkers is to create a shared question that students must work together to answer. The question should be a meaningful or essential question. Essential questions challenge students to employ thoughtful reading, analysis, evaluation, and synthesis of information to create answers, not just find them.[3] Essential questions are interdisciplinary in nature and "probe the deepest issues confronting us" (McKenzie 1997).

One first-grade unit I use essential questions with is the science module "We all grow and change." Science units naturally lend themselves to questioning because science is based on inquiry. In the hallway before students enter I announce our new unit and the essential question we will work together as a community of readers and thinkers to answer: "How do we all grow and change?" I then tell students that the books we will use to answer our essential question are on the table for them to preview.[4] Students file in, return their books, and either make a beeline for the table to be the first to preview or find that "just right" book and meander over to the table later to examine the titles: *The Very Hungry Caterpillar* by Eric Carle, *Egg to Chick* by Millicent Selsam, *A New Frog: My First Look at the Life Cycle of an Amphibian* by Pamela Hickman, *When I Was Five* by Arthur Howard, and *D. W. Thinks Big* by Marc Brown. If I have multiple copies of a title, then each child may have a copy, but it is much more likely that several students will share the same text as they actively read, question, and seek answers together.

As students gather the supplies they need, several glance at the essential question we will use to guide our research and unify our book discussions: "How do we all grow and change?" As a group, we brainstorm additional questions and I add them to our chart. Because students have already previewed the titles we will use in our book clubs, they know that the "we" in the question refers not just to humans but to other living things, like butterflies, frogs, and chicks. Several students who have schema about frogs want to know how a tadpole or polliwog is like a caterpillar, and we all have a giggle attack as we add one student's question: "How are kids like chickens?" But as we come to discover, the growth stages in all four species are quite similar. After we brainstorm the subsidiary questions, groups find a cozy corner in the library to begin reading and asking questions specific to the text they have chosen.[5]

When we gather at the end to share, students summarize for the good of the group the text they have read and ask for help from the whole group with any questions they have not been able to answer. As groups share, I add the answers they have discovered to our chart. Later, students use the information on the chart to create a multimedia presentation showing the similarities and differences in how we all grow and change. Modeling for students how to ask questions and use the group as a resource for answering questions further elevates the level of students' discourse both in their small book club groups and during whole group discussions. The answer to the essential question is the enduring understanding, the overarching principle, which I want students to remember years from now when the details about what develops first on a frog, the hind or front legs, fades.

Categorizing Questions

There are almost as many ways to categorize questions as there are ways to organize the sticky notes students use to record their thinking. Some practitioners recommend categorizing questions into thick or thin. Thick questions are "large global questions"; thin questions are "smaller clarification questions" (Harvey and Goudvis 2000, 90). But years of experience analyzing literature has taught me that in a well-crafted story no detail is extraneous, from the color of the character's clothing to why the author didn't give the character a pet. Reams have been written about James Joyce's use of color imagery; still other critics have linked the absence of pets to the sterility of the modern world in T. S. Eliot's "The Love Song of J. Alfred Prufrock." One student argued that it was Prufrock's lack of connection to anything living that led to his existential angst.

The thick/thin debate came up recently in a discussion with one of my colleagues, a truly gifted second-grade teacher. She had brought the matter up because she had a student who seemed to be stuck asking questions about the unimportant or minor details of a story. When asked for specifics, she recounted that the student wanted to know why the main character in *Aunt Flossie's Hats (and Crab Cakes Later)* was wearing a red dress. "Maybe," I told her, "it's not a minor question. What does the color red symbolize?" "Red is the color of blood," she answered. "In literature it suggests both bravery and sacrifice." She thought about it for a few minutes and said, "Oh. I've got it now. Each of the tales that Aunt Flossie tells is about everyday bravery, survival, and sacrifices." Questions about seemingly minor details can reveal major themes because the text is so sparse in a picture book that every detail counts. Each should be studied with the same care and attention we pay to adult literature.

The same is true of well-crafted chapter books for children. One of the questions that puzzled my second graders as we read *The Case of the Marshmallow Monster* was why Mr. Hancock was described as pear-shaped. When Zachary first asked this question during our group discussion, several students immediately chimed in, "I wondered about that too." One student wanted to know what he looks like if he looks like a pear, so another student sketched his visualization of the character. Clearly, teachers might be initially tempted to dismiss the pear-shaped question as unimportant, but as we analyzed the question we came to see that perhaps the author was revealing his feelings about adults who intentionally try to frighten children. As one of my second graders commented, "You wouldn't describe somebody you liked as pear-shaped."

Even more has been written about encouraging students to devise and divide their questions into Bloom's taxonomy, but, like thick or thin questions, the end result is the same: students spend more time categorizing the questions than they do finding the answers. In addition, Busching and Slesinger note,

> For too long we have used Bloom's Taxonomy to assign artificial values to certain kinds of questions. A hierarchical scheme that values "higher-order" questions over "factual" ones ignores the obvious truth that facts cannot be relegated to a lower order of significance. It is only when facts are the object of isolated, artificially constructed work that they have less to offer the learner. In real inquiry facts offer power and control. The search for an additional fact may be integral to constructing a theory or testing a belief. Facts are both the basis for beliefs and theories and the means for testing them. . . . The outward form of the question may have little to do with the level, the depth, or the importance of thinking that has occurred. (1995, 341)

McKenzie adds:

> The most important questions of all are those asked by students as they try to make sense out of data and information. These are the questions which enable students to Make Up Their Own Minds. Powerful questions—Smart Questions, if you will—are the foundation for Information Power, Engaged Learning and Information Literacy. (1997)

NOTES

1. The glaring exception to the limited value of these questions shows up in historical fiction; knowing where and when the story takes place can help students activate prior knowledge or help identify an information need.

2. Sophisticated readers have learned through experience to tolerate a degree of uncertainty as they read. Fledgling readers, on the other hand, become discouraged and frustrated when they encounter something they do not understand. Teaching children that good readers have questions and how good readers find the answers is essential to developing independent, confident readers and thinkers.

3. For more information on essential questions, read Jamie McKenzie's excellent articles at http://www.fno.org and visit BCPS's online research models built around essential questions at http://www.bcps.org.

4. Much of the research about the benefits of literature circles or book clubs examines the impact on intermediate students, grade 3 and above; however, primary-age students become so excited about being in a club that membership acts as a powerful motivator to develop reading skills.

5. Because valuing students' book choices is critical to engagement, I do not assign students to groups or texts. Students' schema and interest can compensate reading deficits. In addition, all of the texts selected for inclusion in this first-grade book club have text features like diagrams and illustrations that allow all students to access information.

6

Finding
Answers

*You can tell a person
is clever by his/her answers.
You can tell whether a person
is wise by his/her questions.*

Naguib Mahfouz

sking questions is "indispensable for creating and strengthening the reader's ongoing dialogue with the page" (Zimmermann and Hutchins 2003, 71). Learning how to *answer* questions is indispensable for enhancing research skills, deepening comprehension, clarifying thoughts, increasing vocabulary, and enlarging the reader's schema about the world. Learning *how* to find answers transforms the reader from a passive recipient to an active seeker of knowledge. I actively model for students four methods that help readers find answers: Rereading; Reading On; Thinking About; and Consulting a Resource.

Modeling is critical, particularly for my less able readers. Research shows that an

important difference between capable and less capable readers and writers is that those who are less successful are not strategic. They are naïve. They seem reluctant to use unfamiliar strategies and remain dependent on primitive strategies. For example, as they read, less successful readers seldom look ahead or back into the text to clarify misunderstandings or make plans. Or, when they come to an unfamiliar word, they often stop reading, unsure of what to do. They may try to sound out an unfamiliar word, but if that is unsuccessful, they give up. In contrast, capable readers know several strategies, and if one strategy isn't successful, they try another. (Tompkins 2003, 249)

Rereading

Like questioning, rereading is a method that poor readers are at first reluctant to use. Having struggled through a passage once, below-average readers balk at expending the effort and experiencing the frustration again. Only after you show them that good readers reread frequently, and that the second reading is easier than the first, do students begin to see the benefits of rereading.

I model rereading with Cortese's (2004) article, "The Application of Question-Answer Relationship Strategies to Pictures." This is one of many excellent articles about reading, but, like many, it is challenging reading. Because I know that students will have difficulty comprehending the article, I make sure I connect the tactic of rereading to something they already know: riding in a car. "The first time you drive anywhere, you need to keep looking at the directions and signposts; you do not really notice details, like the color of the house on the corner where you turn, particularly if you are driving too fast. The same is true when you read a book for the first time. You are so busy trying to get where you are going that you miss important details. Just like drivers," I tell them, "I have even seen students glancing to see how much farther they have to go. I'm going to read one paragraph from the article aloud at least twice, and I want you to think about how much more you notice the second time through." Then I read aloud from the opening paragraph:

While the majority of comprehension taxonomies assume that questions can be classified as isolated entities, Pearson and Johnson (1978) developed a classification that emphasized the notion that questions do not exist in such a separate manner. They advanced three levels of questioning that are relative to the text to which they refer, as well as to the reader's knowledge base. Rather than consider question types, this perspective views questions by their implied Question-Answer Relationships. Pearson and Johnson defined Question-Answer Relationships as textually explicit (TE) if question and answer are derived from the text and the relationship between the two was explicitly stated, textually implicit (TI) if one step of inference is necessary to answer the question and both question and answer are derived from the text, and scripturally implicit (SI) if a question is derived from the text and the answer is reasonable but nontextual in nature. The Pearson and Johnson taxonomy was the first to highlight the utility of identifying question types according to their relationship to text and reader, and, in doing so, they focused attention on the source of information for comprehension questions—in effect, categorizing a question according to the source of information required for the response. (Raphael 1982; Cortese 2004)

I have copied the opening paragraph onto a transparency, and students gather around the overhead with their sticky notes and pencils. Students observe as I read the first paragraph aloud and listen as I share how confused I felt the first time I read this paragraph. "Normally," I tell my students, "I would ask questions about what I did not understand, but I felt after my first reading that I did not know enough to ask a good question yet." As students nod their heads in agreement and some in sympathy, I reread the passage to pinpoint where comprehension began to break down.[1] As I reread the first sentence, "While the majority of comprehension taxonomies assume that questions can be classified as isolated entities . . . ," I write down several questions: "What are the comprehension taxonomies she is referring to?" "Is it related to Bloom's taxonomy?" "Is the author talking about asking higher-level as opposed to lower-level questions?" "What does 'questions are considered separate entities' mean?" Slowly, I read aloud the next sentence. "Okay. I still am not sure about which comprehension taxonomies she is referring to, but I think the three types Pearson and Johnson created are supposed to be in contrast because of the way the sentence is structured. So if I figure out how they organize questions, then at least I'll know what the strategies are not." I continue to model rereading, questioning and thinking as I make meaning of the passage.

Modeling how to respond to a challenging text is important for two reasons. First, the Maryland State Assessment contains passages that students may have difficulty understanding because either the reading level is too high or they lack the schema to understand the references. The second and more important reason is that in the real world students are confronted by challenging texts all the time, from technical manuals to the not-so-user-friendly manuals that accompany electronic equipment like computers. After we brainstorm what rereading looks and sounds like *and* how rereading helps us to become better readers, students reread for meaning one of the many challenging passages they need to understand to do well on our state assessment test.

Rereading is an effective tactic not only for difficult passages but also for an entire book, as anyone who has ever reread a picture book to a group of children can attest. In addition, the benefits of rereading in increasing comprehension are not limited to just the listening children. Debbie Miller, staff developer extraordinaire and author of *Reading with Meaning: Teaching Comprehension in the Primary Grades* (2002), tells of the time she shared Chris Van Allsburg's *The Stranger* with her first-grade class. One of her students, Grace, asked her, "Mrs. Miller, what are you wondering?" Miller mentioned that she had always wondered what finally made the stranger decide to go, when the child chimed in, "I know why! He had to go because he got his memory back. See the red leaf? Remember how it was green? When he blew on it and it turned red, he got his memory back. See his face? The red leaf made him remember who he was" (2002, 124). Miller wondered how she had missed that detail and still keeps a copy of the book on her desk as a reminder of the benefits of rereading, sharing. and asking questions.

Reading On

Reading on is the second tactic I teach; it entails purposefully resolving to seek answers to questions by continuing to read. As Zimmermann and Hutchins (2003, 76) note, "Sometimes making a conscious decision to keep reading clears up confusion. . . . Having that question in mind as you read on will help you repair the breakdown in understanding." Actively seeking answers to questions as students continue to read is a strategy that proficient readers utilize, knowing that many of the questions will be answered by events that happen later in the text.

This is a tactic my fifth graders effectively employed in their Jean Craighead George book clubs. George is the focus of the author study unit for our fifth graders; in addition, her works address the essential question of the fifth-grade ecology unit: How do human interactions impact the environment? Are the interactions harmful or beneficial?[2] Despite the opportunity to integrate across disciplines, I was still somewhat hesitant to allow students to self-select one of George's books and choose a group to join.

Her books are so rich in details that below-grade-level readers can get lost in the long descriptive passages. In library, students are heterogeneously grouped, so I have gifted and talented students who read well above grade level mixed in with average readers and special education students who are reading well below grade level. In addition, we were limited in book choices, despite the author's prolific output, by the titles available on my library's shelves and by the need to avoid titles that students had already studied extensively in third grade or would study next year in middle school. After factoring in all of these limitations, I had eight titles for students to choose from: *The Case of the Missing Cutthroats: An Ecological Mystery*; *Julie of the Wolves*; *The Missing 'Gator of Gumbo Limbo*; *The Moon of the Wild Pigs*; *One Day in the Desert*; *One Day in the Tropical Rain Forest*; *There's an Owl in the Shower*; and *Who Really Killed Cock Robin? An Ecological Mystery*.

I should have had more faith in the efficacy of comprehension strategies in transforming all of my patrons into active strategic readers.[3] Reading on proved to be an invaluable tactic in allowing students to skim the descriptive passages while purposefully seeking answers to their questions. As I circulated during book discussions, I heard many groups discussing when to use reading on to help them comprehend the story. For example, as I joined one group, three students were discussing which strategy to use to solve their problem: the text had repeatedly referred to an egret, but the girls did not know what an egret was. Jacquanza thought the group should reread; she reasoned that "maybe the egret was important because it was mentioned four times." Lametrice, on the other hand, thought they should read on because "most questions are answered in a few pages anyway." The third girl, Angela, agreed with Lametrice about the value of rereading and pointed out that the group had had the same problem in the previous chapter; they had gotten stuck on the words *armor* and *armadillo*. First they chose to reread the passage, and when that didn't help they had decided to read on; as Angela reminded the group, just three paragraphs later context clues had allowed the girls to figure out not only the meaning of the words but, more important, how George's word choice built the image of the antagonist as a tough, inflexible, alligator hunter.

Obviously, even reading on has its limitations, as able readers already know, but less able readers must be reminded that if one strategy does not work, then try another. I always teach students that, if their questions have not been answered within a few pages in a picture book or by the end of the chapter in a longer text, then they should use one of the two remaining strategies: Thinking About or Consulting a Resource.

Thinking About

Here's an analogy I use with students to help them see why it is so important to stop and think about what they are reading: reading is like putting together a puzzle except that it is even more difficult because you do not have the box top with the picture of the completed puzzle to show you how all of the pieces fit together. "If you want some idea of how difficult reading truly is," I challenge them, "try putting together a puzzle without glancing even once at the picture of the completed puzzle. When you assemble a puzzle, you are so busy trying to figure out how each piece fits that you do not really see the whole until after you have finished." The same is true of reading, especially if the reader has struggled with decoding unfamiliar words or encountered information at dissonance with or outside the realm of his or her schema. "While you are reading you need to stop and think about how the pieces fit together *and* how each piece fits into the big picture the author and you are creating. Thinking about includes inferring and synthesizing the text to understand big ideas or themes in the story." (See chapters 8 and 9 for more information on how to teach these strategies.)

For example, the fifth-grade group studying *The Missing 'Gator of Gumbo Limbo* really had to think about the passage where the main character says, "When we all three lived together, I did many terrible things for which my father hit me. 'Come here, Liza Katherine Poole,' he would shout. I knew when he called me by my full name that I had done something awful and I would tremble." Later in the chapter, Liza says, "I was so very peaceful in the woods in our cozy yellow tent where my father couldn't take off his belt and beat me." Liza stated that she did many terrible things, but were they to believe what the main character said? Sean thought not; he said, "Maybe her father just loses his temper and hits her." Jay agreed and added that he had seen a TV special about abused children where the father had beat the child so badly with a belt that the boy had to be hospitalized, and all the boy had done was spill his milk. Other students in the group initially accepted Liza's statement as fact but came to revise their opinions as they saw through Liza's actions that she was a caring and compassionate person.

Consulting a Resource

Some researchers have suggested categorizing questions according to where the reader would find the answers. Buehl (2001, 106–9) developed question-answer relationships (QARs) to help students actively question the text. In the QAR paradigm, there are two general categories: *In the book* (questions that require use of the text) and *In my head* (questions that draw on the personal experiences of the reader and author). In each category there are two types of question. *In the book* includes Right There questions (answers can be found in one specific place in the text) and Think and Search questions (answers require piecing together different parts of the text). *In my head* includes On My Own questions (answers are related to the reader's personal experiences) and Author and Me questions (answers are related to the reader's personal experiences as well as the author's perspective).

The problem with Buehl's QARs paradigm, as I quickly discovered when I tried this approach with my students, is that frequently the answer was neither in the book nor in their heads. For example, three of my fifth-grade students were struggling over the word *polliwog* in Jean Craighead George's *One Day in the Tropical Rain Forest*. They had used their work attack strategies and had come surprisingly close to the correct pronunciation, but they still didn't know what a polliwog was. The answer was neither in the book nor in their heads. As fledgling readers develop, many of their questions are about vocabulary or about information they need to fill gaps in their background knowledge. In the traditional model of reading instruction, the teacher defines the new vocabulary and supplies the missing background information. If we truly want children to develop as independent readers, then we must teach them how and when to use the wealth of resources in our libraries to find answers.

Consulting a resource is the missing piece in many classrooms where teachers are actively teaching comprehension strategies, but it is critical in enabling students to become actively engaged, strategic, and independent readers. Learning how to find answers in a world where information is increasing exponentially is crucial. According to U.C. Berkeley's School of Information Management and Systems (Lyman and Varian, 2003), five exabytes of information were produced in 2002.[4] Five exabytes is equivalent in size to the information contained in 37,000 libraries the size of the Library of Congress. The growth of information communicated via the Web has been even more dramatic: researchers at the School of Information

Management and Systems estimated the volume of information communicated on the Web in 1999 to be 20–50 terabytes; for 2003, they measured the volume of surface Web information at 167 terabytes—at least triple the previous volume. BrightPlanet estimated the deep Web to be 400–450 times larger.[5] As Leu (2000) notes, "The speed of this change is breathtaking; never before have the technologies of literacy changed so rapidly in such fundamental ways." As the knowledge base continues to increase, students' abilities to stay abreast of new information and to use the information in meaningful ways must become part of our expanded definition of literacy.

At no previous time in human history has the ability to gather, sift, sort, evaluate, and utilize information been so critical, yet literacy textbooks for teachers—at the undergraduate and graduate levels—relegate the role of research to brief suggestions like "research the author or a topic related to the book and present the information as a chart or summary." Part of the fallout from librarians' lack of participation in the dialogue about literacy is that discussions of how to use research in the classroom are limited to a page or less and conclude with the suggestion that teachers develop hot lists of websites for students to visit. Marlene Asselin (2004) tells of presenting a paper on information literacy at a major literacy conference where attendees were surprised by the extant knowledge; they had no idea that numerous resources on information literacy already existed. The attendees at this conference are not an exception from the norm; you would be hard pressed to find a mention of the role of library media specialists in increasing comprehension or teaching information literacy outside the annals of library journals. For example, a search through ProQuest of issues of *The Reading Teacher* from 1988 until the present yielded only two articles about library media specialists.[6] For too long we have been the sage on the sideline, but it is no game we are riding the bench for; instead, it is the critically important task of teaching our students, patrons, and colleagues how to not only locate but also *read* the resources of the global information age.

I divide resources into three types: human, directional, and informational. Human resources are not limited to the peers and colleagues we communicate with daily as we try to make sense of an ever-changing information landscape; they also include content experts and proximally more distant peers who through online discourse become part of the global learning community. Effective communication and collaboration are essential to coping with the explosion of information, particularly in the sciences, and they are the hallmark of "the student who contributes positively to the learning community and to society . . . and participates effectively in groups to pursue and generate information" (ALA 1998, 32). Directional resources are resources that point readers in the direction of the information they seek; directional resources, like the library's catalog or an index, are the tools of the researcher. To use the tools effectively, readers must be able to use a specific subset of discrete skills, like alphabetical ordering and keyword searching. Informational resources are the sources of the content the researcher is seeking. Like all content in every possible format, it must be accessed, evaluated, sorted, synthesized, and utilized in meaningful ways.

Human Resources: Sharing Experiences and Knowledge

The first resource I teach students to use and the favorite of my more sociable students is human resources. I am always amazed by the amount of esoteric knowledge my students possess—one a budding entomologist, another a future historian, and at least three or four paleontologists in training. It is a rare day when at least one student does not have a pertinent experience or background knowledge to share to help answer another student's question. Unfortunately, too many of my students have experience dealing with the death of a loved one, racism, violence, and poverty; their experiences have helped enrich the understanding of many a text and in the process have helped them cope with the problems they are facing.

Students who have read more widely have a larger vocabulary base to share, while other students have experiences taking care of pets or playing a sport—all the knowledge gleaned from following their passions and pursuits. In addition, students' abilities to use context clues and text features as aids to comprehension vary widely, even in a homogeneously grouped class. For example, students in one of the fifth-grade Jean Craighead George book clubs were stuck on an unknown word, *groin*, in *One Day in the Desert*. As I joined their group, they were discussing which strategy to use, and frankly I became just a bit nervous. There was one student in the group whom I had privately dubbed the dictionary diva; she delighted in looking up words and would spend hours, if you let her, browsing the dictionary. In one of those teacher scenarios that immediately unfolds, I could imagine her looking up *groin* and then trying to define *scrotum* and *penis* aloud in a fifth-grade class just after Valentine's Day. Fortunately, another student in the group had reread the passage and used context clues to figure out that the groin is the area of the body between the inner thighs. "Good use of context clues," she graciously said, and I smiled as I thought, "If you only knew."

Interestingly, the group had already had a discussion about how stopping to define every unknown word detracted from their understanding. Unlike other resources, human resources can offer insights that help readers grow and develop by pointing out their strengths and weaknesses. My dictionary diva's group members had suggested that instead of interrupting her reading every time she encountered an unfamiliar word she try reading on or using context clues. In addition to using context clues, peers have offered valuable advice like, "You may want to slow down and think about what you are reading," and my favorite, "You may want to choose books about another topic to broaden your schema," to the child who persistently checks out only dinosaur books. Other benefits are evident in students' sticky notes.

The other human resource students know to consult is their friendly librarian, but I know that I must walk a fine line between helping them become independent readers and researchers and fulfilling the critical role of the librarian as an information portal. As a school library media specialist, it is my job to model how to locate, access, and evaluate information found on our shelves and beyond. I teach students that reference librarians can answer specific research-related questions and show them how to use services like Ask a Librarian to find answers. Their favorite is Maryland Ask Us Now! (a 24/7 online interactive service that uses trained librarians to

When I get stuck, I can ask a question.

It helped me become a better thinker because I did not know which details and main idea I should take out of the book.
—Peter F.

provide answers to students' questions) because of the live chat format. Students also regularly consult the many Ask an Expert resources available on the Web.

We use the same criteria for evaluating the usefulness of human resources as we do for print and online resources: accuracy, authority, currency, objectivity/bias, and coverage. That human sources of information must be evaluated by the same criteria we use for other resources is one of the most powerful and useful lessons I can ever teach my students. Think of all the tragic incidents and conflicts in history that could have been avoided if people were trained to ask: Is the person sharing the information authoritative and reliable? What biases does the person sharing the information have? Why are they sharing the information? Is this information timely and accurate? Does the information agree with what I read or already know about the topic?

Directional Resources: Learning How to Use the Tools of the Researcher

Finding answers is sometimes as simple as knowing where to look, so next I model for students how to use directional resources like the library catalog, bibliographies, indexes, hierarchal subject guides, electronic databases, and search engines. Students must be taught how to use the tools of the researcher if they are to become successful seekers of knowledge. Knowing which search engine to use and how to use advanced search features saves students time and frustration. In a world dominated by the supremacy of a few popular search engines like Google, it comes as quite a shock, not only to my students but also to my colleagues, that there are subject-specific search engines, like Vivisimo BioMed, and search engines for specific information needs, like the TIGER Map service for U.S. census information.

Although there are differences in how the researcher finds information in each of these resources, the general principles for finding information are the same with a library's catalog, an electronic database, or an Internet search engine. Teaching students the basics of keyword, subject tree, and Boolean search techniques helps them transfer these skills to the use of other library catalogs, newly acquired databases, and the ever-changing list of search engines. After learning how to use directional resources to find information, students are able to pursue their questions independently and consult me or one of the other human resources described above if they encounter difficulties.

Informational Resources: Using Authentic Questions

Violet Harada (2003) describes a collaborative partnership between library media specialist Debora Lum and kindergarten teacher Kathy Souza. Lum and Souza joined forces to examine how kindergarten students conducted an inquiry-focused project; they found that student-generated questions were central to the inquiry process. Souza's kindergarteners had generated questions about a strange bug they had found on the playground. They naturally wanted to know if the bug was poisonous or might bite them, a very real-world information need. Souza's students decided that the best place to begin their research was the library media center, and so they went to Lum for help. They combed the library shelves together but were unsuccessful, so Lum suggested that the team contact a "bug expert." They loved the idea. Souza helped them photograph the bug, and they sent the digital image along with the following e-mail message to an entomologist at the local university:

> Der Mr. Kumashiro:
>
> We fownd a bug on the sidwok at or school. It is red and black. It has 2 antennae and small squares on its back. Kan you hlp us? We want to no if this bug is dangris and if it pichas and what it can do. Can you tell us its name too?

The kindergarteners were quite excited when the entomologist replied that the insect was an assassin bug and that it could bite people. Armed with this information, students were able to discover other resources and learn many more facts about the assassin bug, which they eagerly shared with their classmates.

Authentic inquiry such as Harada describes begins with questions students generate as a result of their experiences, including the texts they choose to read. The questions students cannot answer by rereading, reading on, or consulting a human resource are natural starting points for research. A single group of students might decide to conduct research during their group meeting, or more likely I might schedule a research session when, based on conferences with groups, several groups need to consult information sources. As a result, I might have students pursuing twenty-five different lines of questioning on topics as diverse as how many children are homeless in America and what the restrictions are on hunting alligators in the Florida Everglades. Queries range from the simple (like definitions of unfamiliar terms) to the complex (such as how humans impact fragile ecosystems like the Everglades).

Informational Resources: Learning How to Evaluate and Use the Information

Leu, Mallette, and Karchmer (2001) suggest what librarians have long known: "Literacy, technology, and literacy instruction are quickly converging. Thus, teachers are challenged not only to integrate technology with traditional aspects of literacy instruction (i.e., book and paper-pencil reading and writing) but also to engage students in emerging technological literacies." Information literacy is the information base for the other twenty-first-century literacies: "visual, historical, cultural, political and news media, technical, scientific and mathematical" (Abilock 2004). For example, you could not be science literate in today's society without the ability to gather, sift, sort, analyze, evaluate, and synthesize the vast array of new information produced each day in the sciences.

In addition, the cornerstones of the new literacies, basic (language) literacy and information literacy, are becoming increasingly intertwined. For students to be successful they must be able to use information literacy to locate authoritative, current resources independently at their reading level *and* use basic language literacy to comprehend the resources they have located. The ability to locate information is useless if students cannot understand what they have found; similarly, the ability to read is ineffectual if students lack the skills to obtain the background knowledge they need to understand the text. The same comprehension strategies (connecting, questioning, finding answers, visualizing, determining importance, inferring, synthesizing, and using fix-up strategies) we use for print must be applied to online and nonprint resources.[7]

Third-grade students developed their twenty-first-century literacy skills while researching current threats to the rain forest. We began the unit by reading *The Great Kapok Tree: A Tale of the Amazon Rain Forest* by Lynne

Cherry. Students actively questioned the text as I read it aloud. One of their questions was, "How old is the book?" What they wanted to know was how timely the information was; they knew any information in the sciences that is over five years old must be considered out of date. Using the five-year cutoff date for science-related topics is the first (and easiest) way they sift information. We looked at the copyright and discovered that the book was published in 1990, well beyond our cutoff date, so our first question was "What is the state of the rain forest now?" Additional questions soon followed: "Is the rain forest more or less endangered than it was fifteen years ago?" "Which threat to the rain forest is the most dangerous today?" "Are the animals, people, and plants of the rain forest in as much danger as when Cherry first wrote the book?"

Students overwhelmingly chose online resources to find the answers to their questions because of the need to obtain current information; in addition, the use of technology motivates students to dig deeper and helps to scaffold their research. For example, students began their research by consulting a general reference source, *The New Book of Knowledge Online*. They entered "rain forest" in the search box because they needed general background knowledge about rain forests. Students have been taught to use the same tools (Table of Contents and Index) and text features (subheadings, captions, illustrations, graphs and other graphics) online as they do to gain meaning from print resources. Teaching how to use tools and text features to find the information they need quickly is important for all students, but it is critically important for below-grade-level readers who become frustrated and disengaged by large blocks of text not related to their information needs. Students either click on the Table of Contents and then click on the subheading "Threats to Rain Forests" or scroll down the page to that section of the article.

After students have located the pertinent portion of the article, they copy and paste the section into Microsoft Word in order to use technology as a tool to scaffold their reading. Like the majority of general reference articles, the "Rain Forests" article they find is well above the average elementary student's reading level. The Flesch-Kincaid Grade Level for the article is a 10.3, which means that an average student in the third month of the tenth-grade year can easily read the article.[8] To help students understand the main idea of the article, the first thing students do is select the AutoSummarize option under the Tools menu. By default, AutoSummarize is set to reduce the article to 25 percent of the original by summarizing the key points. After students have read the shortest summary available, they incrementally increase the amount of text summarized to at least 50 percent of the original text. By gradually increasing the amount of text displayed, students are more easily able to discriminate between the main idea and supporting details, which assists struggling readers who frequently focus on interesting details at the expense of the big picture. (See chapter 7 for more information about helping students identify the main idea.)

Other tools in Microsoft Word help students find information and make meaning. For example, I show students how to use the Find feature (in the Edit menu) to locate their keywords within the article quickly. In chapter 3, I described how students in second grade and above use the Insert Comment feature to annotate articles, while younger students insert voice comments to record their thinking. Finally, students can right-click (or Control-click, on a Mac) any word they do not know to obtain a list of synonyms. In the rain forest exercise (see figure 6-1), students right-clicked on *sustain*, a word they did not recognize; the list of synonyms that appeared helped them determine that *sustain* means *continue*. If they did not

FIGURE 6-1

Using Comprehension Strategies Online with "Threats to Rain Forests"

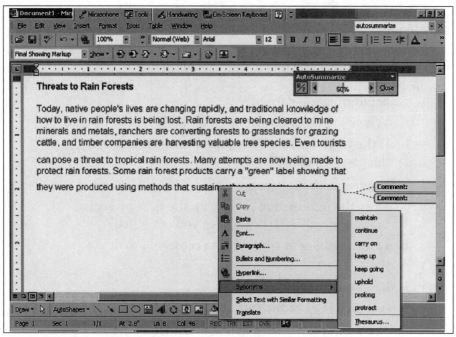

recognize any of the synonyms listed, they could click on the Thesaurus link to look up the word. Identifying synonyms not only helps students make meaning but also aids in the development of vocabulary.

After students use a general reference resource to build their schema, they are ready to delve deeper to find answers to their questions. To locate books, magazine and newspaper articles, TV and radio transcripts, and websites, students choose from one of three directional resources: the library catalog, the portal for the fee-based databases our county subscribes to, or a search engine. Allowing students to choose which resource to use is just as important as allowing them the autonomy to self-select texts.

Once they have chosen the directional resource, students select the type(s) of search they will conduct first: keyword, Boolean, or subject tree. For example, several students chose to use SIRS Discoverer because they could pre-sift results by date and reading level; in addition, they could easily use Boolean logic to refine their results because the Boolean operators, like the search box, are at the top of the results page. That way, instead of wading through the hundreds of results their peers had returned, they had only eight, and all of them were timely, topical, and accessible to an average third-grade reader. A handful of students prefer to use print resources, so they used the library catalog to locate books published within the past five years. Still other students chose to use a search engine because the interactive, multimedia components of many websites help them access content.

No matter which resource students choose, they know that all information sources must be evaluated by the same criteria:

1. Is the information current?
   a. When was the information published?
   b. If the topic is related to science, is the date within the past five years?[9]
2. Is the information accurate?
   a. Does the information agree with the facts presented in the general reference source you consulted?
   b. Does anything in your schema cause you to doubt the accuracy?
3. Is the information objective?
   a. Are the biases of the author or organization clearly stated?
   b. Are several sides presented in a balanced way?

4. Is the information authoritative?

   a. Is the author clearly identified? Is background information, like a brief biography, included?

   b. What training or credentials does the author have?

   c. What clues does the URL give you about the authority of the source?

5. How user friendly is the information source?

   a. Is the information at your reading level?

   b. Does the information source contain tools like a Table of Contents, Index, or Site Map or an internal search engine?

   c. Does the information source use text features like subheadings, captions, and illustrations or other graphics to highlight key points?

Once students have evaluated their information sources, they are ready to use the information in meaningful ways as they find and extend the answers to their questions.

Leu (2000) notes,

> The technologies of literacy involve each of us; we must change our focus as rapidly as the technologies of literacy themselves change. Anything less will shortchange our children, denying them important opportunities during their journeys through life. Change happens in the technologies of literacy; change must also happen throughout the literacy education community.

As full partners in the literacy education community, librarians must work to ensure that our patrons are able to use comprehension strategies, information literacy, and technology effectively to access content, scaffold reading, and present the results of their research if they and we are to be successful.

NOTES

1. One student actually asked, "Is that a 'just right' text for you, Ms. Grimes?"
2. One of the ways I find the additional time to teach comprehension strategies is by integration, integration, and still more integration; through the Jean Craighead George book clubs I integrated reading comprehension strategy instruction, author study (including identifying key elements of the author's

craft), habitat explorations, and research skills as students sifted through currents events to identify threats to the environment. What began as a curricular necessity now results in a richer and more authentic reading experience.

3. Do keep in mind that your patrons, like mine, are receiving ongoing instruction in phonics, phonemic awareness, vocabulary, and fluency.

4. An exabyte is a billion gigabytes, or 10^{18} bytes. A terabyte is a thousand gigabytes, or 10^{12} bytes.

5. The *surface web* refers to fixed web pages, those accessed by search engines such as Google. The *deep web* refers to content in online, usually fee-based databases that general web crawlers cannot reach because the content is dynamic and retrieved in real time as the result of a direct query.

6. Thinking there might be a problem with my search terms, I changed "library media specialist" to "librarian" and again searched back issues of *The Reading Teacher*. At first the results looked slightly more encouraging—ten articles were returned—until I realized that four of the results were reviews of one book, *The Librarian Who Measured the Earth*.

7. To find resources at their reading level, I have taught students to use electronic databases, like Electric Library or SIRS Discoverer, where they can search for resources not only by keyword but also by reading level; or they might use a search engine like KidsClick! which also specifies the reading level. Another resource where reading ability does not pose a barrier is BrainPOP, the producer of online animated, educational videos.

8. To easily determine the readability of an article you have copied into Microsoft Word, simply click on Spelling and Grammar under the Tools menu. Click on the Options button and select Show Readability Statistics. When Word has finished spell-checking the document, a pop-up window displays the Flesch Reading Ease Score and the Flesch-Kincaid Grade Level. Note: You must have a spelling error somewhere in the document for the statistics to appear, so I usually just put an X at the end of the article to activate the readability feature.

9. There are obvious exceptions to the five-year guideline, times when the information must be much more current. For example, my third-grade students were participating in a research project to choose the landing site for the next Mars Rover mission. On March 2, 2004, just as they were completing their research, data from the rover Opportunity revealed the presence of water in Eagle Crater in the distant past. Students had to access the new information rapidly and revise their suggestions in light of the new data. I have rarely seen students so excited; they willingly gave up recess and spent time after school examining the implications of Opportunity's discovery. They felt, they told me, like real scientists because they were plugged in to the same information sources that scientists around the world were using.

7
Determining Importance

I don't read
such small stuff
as letters;
I read men
and nations.

Sojourner Truth

s librarians and teachers, we all have stories to tell of the child who when asked to summarize a story takes a deep breath and retells word by word, detail after detail, the entire story. Similarly, each of us has seen children who when asked to highlight the main idea submit papers that could nearly glow in the dark from the sheer amount of fluorescent yellow marker used to highlight almost everything on the page.[1] Both groups of children suffer from the inability to determine importance, to distinguish between main ideas or themes and supporting details. Harvey and Goudvis (2000, 119) note that "the ability to identify essential ideas and salient information is a prerequisite to developing insight." In addition, determining what is important in fiction and nonfiction is critical to comprehension and retention. Children awash in a sea of details cannot identify and thus comprehend main ideas or themes. Nor can they effectively summarize and commit to memory what is important to retain and recall. Just as important, as the *Report of the National Reading Panel* notes, "Strategies such as inferring, visualizing, and synthesizing are all predicated on the assumption that a reader is capable of differentiating between what is significant and what is secondary in a text" (NICHD 2000).

The ability to determine importance in fiction and nonfiction clearly differentiates my poor from my proficient readers. Poor readers become lost in the minutiae of the story or confuse supporting details with the main ideas in nonfiction. They are unable to identify what a story shows, not merely tells; in retelling a story, they include every detail no matter how insignificant. In nonfiction, they focus on details, like the fact that a hammerhead can grow over 11.5 feet in length, while missing the main idea: hammerheads, like other types of sharks, are increasingly becoming an endangered species just as scientists are learning how sharks may save lives by unlocking the clues to resisting diseases, including AIDS.

My proficient readers, on the other hand, effectively utilize both text structures and features to summarize and identify the main ideas or themes. Text structure is the organizational matrix, like cause and effect, the author chooses to craft his or her work. Text features are the headings, font styles, pullouts, sidebars, and illustrations used to highlight key ideas. Both Weaver and Kintsch (1991) and Seidenberg (1989) note "that 'awareness' of text structure benefits reading comprehension of global ideas, or main theses or ideas" (cited by Dickson, Simmons, and Kameenui 1995). The evidence for the effectiveness of teaching readers how to utilize text structures is so compelling that Pearson and Fielding (1991, 832) cited the benefit of "just about any" type of instruction in expository text structure.

Dickson, Simmons, and Kameenui (1995) synthesized research over the past two decades on determining importance and found that, not only does the ability to comprehend main ideas distinguish good from poor readers, but it is also directly related to general comprehension ability (citing Seidenberg 1989).[2] In addition, they noted that "a major contribution of research has been to transform reading skills (e.g., summarize, identify main ideas, and identify relations between main ideas) into explicit strategies that students can be taught directly." Poor readers can be taught how to use the following:

The text's physical presentation (e.g., location of topic sentences, headings, subheadings, signal words), to identify main ideas and form relations between concepts, main ideas, and supporting details

The story grammar, to identify important ideas in the text

Expository text structures, to identify concepts and relations or to impose relations on poorly written text

The missing component in the above listing is the piece that librarians are particularly well qualified to teach: determining importance by sifting, sorting, and analyzing information. Determining importance, locating the big ideas in fiction and nonfiction, cannot be reduced to utilizing the sub-headings, locating the climax in a story, or recognizing that an expository passage uses cause and effect to organize the text—although each is an important aid in locating main ideas. Despite what real estate agents tell us, it is not all about location, location, and location. Finding approximately where in the text the main ideas should be is an important first step, but it is just that, the first step. Similarly, knowing where to look for clues to themes is essential, but it is only the beginning phase of understanding the rich, multifaceted themes that underpin the body of children's literature. Discerning the big ideas in fiction and nonfiction is a thoughtful process, one that must be modeled repeatedly and with a wide variety of texts.

Determining Important Ideas in Fiction

I use Leo Lionni's *Swimmy* as a bridge between the strategies of finding answers and the new strategy I will introduce to my first graders today: determining importance. *Swimmy* is the story of how one little black fish survives tragedy, loneliness, and rejection to find a new community, only to see it threatened by imminent danger. The previous week, students had independently asked questions and found answers as I read Lionni's picture book aloud. Assessment of their responses indicated that all students had achieved at least a satisfactory level of strategy implementation. Today I read *Swimmy* aloud again, but with a new focus: finding the big ideas or themes.

Using a familiar text helps students to focus on what is truly a higher-order thinking task. Although there is no hierarchy for the strategies proficient readers use, there is a continuum.[3] Connecting is at the beginning of the continuum; it is the easiest strategy for students to learn to employ because it is how we learn. Connecting what we learn to what we know is how humans organize and store incoming information. Determining importance is near the other end of the continuum because of the degree of abstract reasoning required.

I use fiction to introduce determining importance because research suggests that students recognize, comprehend, and remember narrative structures easier than they do expository structures (Graesser, Golding, and

Long 1991; Zabrucky and Ratner 1992). Even though utilizing narrative structure is easier for children, identifying themes in fiction is still challenging because it requires the ability to identify the story elements, including correctly recognizing the main character, setting, plot, conflict, and resolution; and to conceptualize abstract concepts like friendship, survival, and community.

As students gather their thinking paraphernalia (pencils, sticky notes, and clipboards), they glance curiously at the display—"What's the big idea?"—on our thinking board. Usually the thinking board contains a definition of the strategy we will focus on that day, or it is used to post evidence of the critical thinking children have been doing throughout the week. "Today," I tell my first graders, "I am going to model how good readers determine the big ideas in fiction. The big ideas, or themes, are the reason we study stories in school. The big ideas show us important ideas like the meaning of friendship and community. Themes teach us important lessons about life, like how to survive against nearly impossible odds, or that most differences between people are only skin deep. Ideas are not things you can see, touch, hear, or taste, so the author has to *show* us ideas through the actions and reactions of the main characters to what happens to them and around them. Because the author does not tell us the theme directly, I really have to pay attention and think about what the main character does, says, feels, and thinks. Your job is to observe and record what determining the big ideas looks and sounds like so that we can use your great thinking to create a checklist for us to use when it's your turn to find the theme."

I begin by previewing the title. "Titles are important clues to themes, so I know that Lionni's title is telling me to pay attention to a main character named Swimmy and all of the things that happen to him." Next I examine the cover illustration. "When I'm looking for clues to themes, I know it is really important to pay attention to the description of the character, including how the character looks and acts. Swimmy looks different than the other fish; he is black and the other fish are red. Also, Swimmy is swimming all by himself ahead of all of the other fish. I think how he looks and acts are important clues, so I'm going to record that on my sticky note." Children observe as I code the sticky note DI for determining importance, add -CC for character clues, and then record my observations.[4]

Now I begin rereading *Swimmy* aloud. I stop after the first page and say, "I know that what happens in the beginning, middle, and end of the story are important in summarizing the story and thinking about the themes, so I'm going to write down what happens in the beginning on my sticky note. Now, my sticky note is small, so I know I can write down only the most important things that happen: Swimmy escapes when a tuna comes and eats his whole family because he can swim faster than his brothers and sisters." I code the note B, for beginning, and say, "Now, instead of putting the sticky note summarizing the beginning here on the first page, I'm going to put it at the end of the story to remind me to compare what happens in the beginning with what happens at the end of the story. I'll do the same when I get to the middle of the book. Thinking about what happens in the beginning, middle, and end will help me summarize the story and identify the themes."

"Next," I continue, "I know that when something important happens, like Swimmy's entire family is eaten, I need to pay attention to how the main character looks, acts, and feels." "Swimmy feels scared, sad, and lonely," I write on a sticky note. Again I code the note DI-CC for determining importance–character clue and return to thinking aloud. "He also feels different from everyone else; not only is he black, but also he can swim faster than anyone else, which is why he escaped. I wonder if that makes Swimmy feel happy, sad, or both?" I add that Swimmy feels different because of his color and his ability to swim faster to the sticky note.

Next I say, "Wow. I've only read the first page and look at all the problems the main character has. I know that the problems the character faces are the most important clues about themes. Let me think about what each problem shows. I think that, because Swimmy feels sad and lonely, one big idea is that fish and people need family and friends. I'm also thinking that, because Swimmy feels scared and sad, another theme might be that you need to enjoy life because you never know when it might end. That's a really big idea, one that I think I'll keep thinking about long after I finish reading the story."

I look back at my sticky note and say, "Hmmm, I wonder what the author is trying to show me about being different. I'm thinking that Lionni could be showing me that being different is a good thing because swimming faster than everyone else allowed Swimmy to escape, and a bad thing because now he feels sad and lonely. I wonder if Lionni is saying that being different is a mixed blessing, good and bad at the same time? I need to keep thinking about what being different means as I read the rest of the story."

I stop and invite children to share what determining importance in fiction looks and sounds like:[5]

"You do a lot of thinking and wondering."

"Yeah, you said I think and I wonder a lot."

"Your face gets all squinty and you look really mean, but you're not. You're just thinking hard."

"You think about how the main character looks, acts, and feels."

"You think about the title too; you know, the clues the title gives you."

"You look at and think about the picture on the cover."

"You pay attention to what happens to the main character."

"You think about the big ideas the problems show you."

"You write down what happened in the beginning on one little sticky note."

"Yeah, and then you stick the note at the end of the book."

I write down their responses on large chart paper children can refer to as we practice determining ideas together, with a peer, and independently. One common denominator in their responses that children immediately notice is how frequently the word "think" appears. Identifying the main character, the plot, and the conflict or problems is the first and easiest step in determining importance; modeling for children how to think about what each of those elements shows us is the next step. Teaching children to identify the main character or conflict is easy, which may explain why the majority of instruction focuses on these discrete skills. Teaching children to think is much more challenging; it requires frequent modeling and the willingness on the part of teachers to allow children to see us as authentic readers who make mistakes, are sometimes confused, and do not immediately recognize every vocabulary word there is to know.

Together, we think through the next few pages where Swimmy's actions show us that one way to overcome grief and sadness is to observe the natural beauty in the world around us and to allow time for healing to occur. We code these notes DI-L for determining importance–learned; the underlined L is a code they are familiar with from their KWL charts.[6] And together, we craft a summary of the middle of the book: "Swimmy is happier as he observes all the wonders in the world, but he is still lonely until he meets another school of fish." We place this second summary at the end of the book too.

Next I have the children turn and face each other knee to knee. So far in the lesson I have been doing the modeling and guiding; now it is time to allow children to begin to employ the strategy with the assistance of a peer. It will take another six to eight weeks before all students are able to determine importance independently. Gradually releasing the onus of using the strategy to them is the only way of assuring that they will be able to use it flexibly and independently. Their job as I read the last third of the book aloud is to think about and record on sticky notes the character clues and what we learn as a result of how Swimmy acts, looks, and feels about problems he encounters.[7] I pause at the end of each page to give children the opportunity to think about, discuss, and record their insights. As always, I circulate and listen in on their discussions. At the end of the book, I give them slightly longer (three to four minutes) to collaborate on their summary. We will use their summaries shortly to think about the main theme, the one test makers ask about in a series of selected response items, but first I ask students to share the big ideas they have learned from how the character looks, acts, and feels about his problems:

- It doesn't matter what color your skin is.
    DI-CC: "Swimmy is black and the other fish are red."

- Even if you're little, you can defeat somebody bigger.
    DI-CC: "Swimmy and the other fish scare away the bigger fish."

- You can do more if you work with others.
    DI-CC: "They all work together to pretend they are bigger than the scary fish."

- You can scare away somebody bigger by being smart.
    DI-CC: "Swimmy is smart! He thinks to tell all the other fish how to look like one big fish."

- It's better to have friends than be by yourself.
    DI-CC: "Swimmy is happy when he finds other fish to be his friends."

As I praise their smart thinking, I reflect that my praise is not a reflexive reaction or hollow congratulations. As always, I am amazed by the wonderful thinking my first graders can do once they are shown how. Each of the themes they share contains practical advice for living and invaluable insights into the human condition. Denigrating any of these insights by forcing children to choose the main idea or theme is the exact opposite of what we should be attempting to accomplish, but I would be doing my students a grave disservice if I did not. Too much rides on how well children perform on high-stakes tests for me not to prepare them to answer questions about *the* main idea or theme. So I tell my students that among all of these great insights, the one the test makers are looking for is the one that links the beginning, middle, and end of the story. I give each child a "What's the Big Idea?" handout and have them place their beginning, middle, and end summaries in the first box (figure 7-1).

Simply moving their sticky notes avoids the tedium and time wasted in recopying. Next we move all of the sticky notes we coded DI-L to the middle box, then we think about which of the many things we learned links the beginning, middle, and end of the story. The first character clue we wrote down is that Swimmy looks different from the other fish; he is black and the other fish are red. We learned from this that "skin color does not matter"; it's a really important idea, but it is not included in the middle of the story, so we place this insight on the bottom of the lightbulb. So too do we sift out the theme about dealing with grief; though an important insight and a comforting thought, it only occurs in the middle of the story. We continue to sift through, think about, and combine our remaining insights until we create one that is true in the beginning, middle, and end of the story: "People need to work together as a community [from the end] or they will be lonely [from the middle] and defenseless [from the beginning]." We record this main theme on the lines in the top of the lightbulb and staple our remaining sticky notes in place. To show students that each of their insights is as valuable as *the* theme test makers are looking for, in the next lesson children will use Kid Pix Deluxe, 3rd Edition, to illustrate their insights by drawing the main character's actions, feelings, and thoughts that were the clues to the big ideas children identified.

Determining Importance in Nonfiction

Traditionally, identifying main ideas and themes are considered separate skills. Main idea is taught for nonfiction and theme is taught for fiction, and never the twain should meet. But the traditional view ignores the obvious: there are themes in nonfiction and main ideas in fiction. Both

FIGURE 7-1

"What's the Big Idea" Worksheet

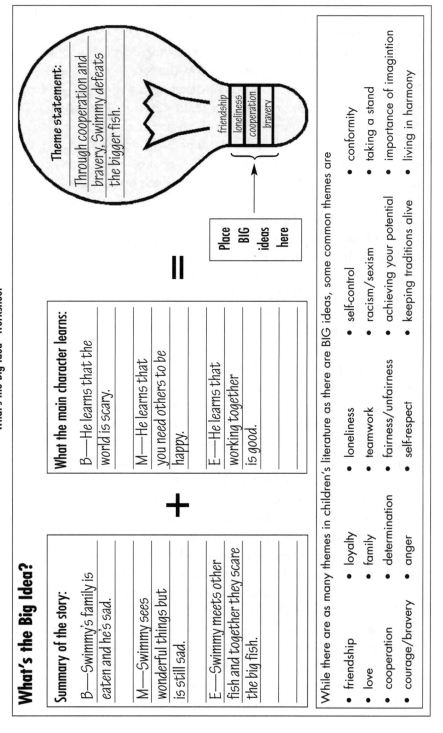

What's the Big Idea?

Summary of the story:

B—Swimmy's family is eaten and he's sad.

M—Swimmy sees wonderful things but is still sad.

E—Swimmy meets other fish and together they scare the big fish.

+

What the main character learns:

B—He learns that the world is scary.

M—He learns that you need others to be happy.

E—He learns that working together is good.

=

Place BIG ideas here

Theme statement:

Through cooperation and bravery, Swimmy defeats the bigger fish.

friendship
loneliness
cooperation
bravery

While there are as many themes in children's literature as there are BIG ideas, some common themes are

- friendship
- love
- cooperation
- courage/bravery

- loyalty
- family
- determination
- anger

- loneliness
- teamwork
- fairness/unfairness
- self-respect

- self-control
- racism/sexism
- achieving your potential
- keeping traditions alive

- conformity
- taking a stand
- importance of imagintion
- living in harmony

81

contain big ideas, and, for both, it's knowing where to look and how to determine importance.

In nonfiction, readers look at text features and text structures. "Text structures," I tell my students, "are how the text is constructed. It's like the building materials that go into constructing a building. The builder uses wood, nails, steel, and concrete to build a house. Text structures are embedded in the text, much like how the framework for the house is covered by bricks and plaster. To build the framework for the text, the expository writer uses cause and effect, narrative, sequence, comparison and contrast, enumeration, description, or persuasion. Each text structure comes with a blueprint or plan for organizing the text, and the writer uses different tools for each. For example, the writer uses the words *first*, *second*, and *third* as tools to build a sequence structure. These tools provide semantic clues for the reader. If I see the phrase *on the other hand* or *by comparison*, I know the writer is using comparison and contrast, so I need to look for the ideas being contrasted. Unlike fiction, where the author *shows you*, nonfiction writers structure their writings so that the first or second sentence *tells you* what is important."

"Text features, on the other hand, are like the finishing touches the interior decorator uses once the builder is finished to accent certain features. Text structures are constructed by the writer, but text features are usually added by someone else like the editor or the production design team. It's much easier to find and use text features to determine importance than text structures, because text features are designed to call attention to an important idea. Poor readers, however, do not use text features; they skip reading headlines and pull-out quotes. They ignore sidebars, graphs, and illustrations. It's like they think, 'If it's not in the body of the text, then it can't be important.' Good readers use text features even before they begin reading the text. They preview the text features just like we preview the title and cover illustration. They scan titles and subheadings first. They look for boldface print and italics. They examine the sidebars, graphs, and illustrations before they begin reading. And they preview text supports, like the Table of Contents or the Glossary."

"Today," I tell my fifth-grade students, "we are going to use text features and structures to determine the important ideas in *Brain and Nerves* by Steve Parker. Your job is think about and record what using text features and structures looks like and how it helps us determine important ideas." Fifth graders are studying body systems in science; in library we are focusing on how the brain and nervous system work, including the physiological functions, cognition, and memory as well as brain injuries and diseases. Comprehension strategies, like determining importance, need to be modeled not only in the reading classroom and library media center but also in the science, social studies, and mathematics classrooms. Later, students will synthesize their findings in a picture book they write and illustrate; their picture books are then donated to local hospital pediatric emergency rooms to provide reading materials that explain in kid-friendly language what's happening inside sick or injured bodies.

I begin by previewing the Table of Contents and notice immediately that the chapters seem to be grouped by what the nervous system is, how it works, and what can go wrong. I comment on how knowing how the text is organized helps me become a better reader. I also notice that there is a Glossary on page 31 to help me if I need it. I turn to page 6, where the Table of Contents tells me the section on the nervous system begins. As I turn the pages, I note how using text supports like the Table of Contents has helped me immediately go to the information I need.[8] Next I examine the illustration that shows not only the brain and spinal cord, which I knew to be part of the nervous system, but also the ganglia and the ulnar, digital, sciatic, and tibial nerves. I immediately code a sticky note DI-<u>L</u>, note that "The nervous system extends throughout the entire body, even to the toes!" and share that, without looking at the illustration, I am not sure I would have understood how extensive the nervous system is.

Then I examine a graphic that shows a girl sniffing a flower and a boy getting ready to swing a baseball bat. I pay attention to how the two children look and note that the girl is dressed in a pink top and matching skirt while the boy is wearing a sweatshirt and baseball cap. I wonder aloud if the text is biased and if it stereotypes boys and girls. I code a sticky note DI and write "Check for bias." Too many of my children equate science with unassailable truth, not realizing that science has been used and misused as justification for everything from sexual discrimination to the infamous Tuskegee syphilis study—the federal experiment that traced the course of the disease in over four hundred African American men who were not informed that they had a treatable sexually transmitted disease. Simply knowing that the text may be biased makes me a more critical reader. Even if the existence of a bias in our book is confirmed, I still share that text with my students. If we pre-screen and pre-sanitize everything children read, then they are ill equipped to detect bias when they encounter it while reading independently.

Next I examine the text in a graphic critically and note that "The information in the graphic compares and contrasts information traveling to and from the brain." I point out the semantic clues, like the phrase *as well as*, which signal that the author is using comparison and contrast. Then I talk about how comparing and contrasting how information travels to and from the brain helps me understand how the nervous system functions.

Finally, I look at the body of text, but I am still not ready to read it in its entirety. I model for students how to scan the text. "Scanning," I tell them, "is like taking a picture walk through a picture book or previewing the title, cover illustration, and Table of Contents. It's looking at the whole text and trying to find the clues to the text structure so that I can use the structure to help me understand what I am reading. In addition to scanning for structure, I am looking for semantic clues, or signal words, that tell me the type of structure the author used. The first thing I notice when I scan the text is that it is one really long paragraph filled with words I do not know, like *autonomic* and *sciatic*. The next details I notice are semantic clues like *second* and *a third part*. The clues tell me that the author is using either sequence or enumeration to structure his writing. I think that the structure is most likely enumeration, because sequence is usually broken up into steps, like directions for baking a cake. Knowing which structure the author is using helps me feel more confident about tackling such a long and challenging paragraph. The paragraph is so long because the author is simply listing all of the parts of the nervous system, and the words I don't know are probably the different parts."

Students now observe as I skim the text. "Skimming is reading selected portions of the text; the part of the text you select to read depends on the type of text structure the author used. Parker uses enumeration, so the most important information should be in the first or second sentence. The rest of the paragraph should enumerate or list all the different parts of the nervous system. When you are not sure which text structure the author used, it is always smart thinking to read the first two sentences; expository writers almost always place the topic sentence, which contains the main idea for the paragraph, in the first or second sentence." I read the first two sentences aloud: *The biggest and most important part of the body's nerve network is the brain. It tapers at its base into the spinal cord, which lies inside the backbone.* Of the two sentences, I tell my students, the first definitely contains the main idea; the second sentence simply adds more details. I write that down, but I put a question mark next to it until I finish reading the entire passage. I code a sticky note DI-?MI (for main idea) and write "The most important part of the nervous system is the brain."

Before I read the entire passage, I invite students to share what they have observed so far and how using text features and structures as well as scanning and skimming help us become better readers. Some of the most insightful comments come from my students who are learning disabled (LD), or for whom English is a second language. For example, one of my LD children said that he would have given up when he saw that long paragraph filled with words he didn't know; he was excited to know that good readers, like me, felt the same way and that there were things you could do when you felt overwhelmed. Other readers were equally excited that they could use the graphics for clues to determine meaning and importance before they began reading. I found it quite interesting that somewhere along the way, probably in the transition from picture books to more challenging texts, many of these children had gathered the erroneous impression that mature readers did not use picture clues. I knew that they had once used picture clues effectively, because one of the many joys of working in the library is seeing these readers evolve over the years I have the pleasure of teaching them. Others commented that they had never thought of scanning the text first to look for text structures, so I knew that one of the many follow-up lessons would be about what the various text structures are and how to use them effectively. One student was simply amazed that any book other than a textbook had a Table of Contents; I like to think she was absent when I covered that extensively in second grade! Though it is possible she was absent, it is much more likely that she, like the rest of us, needs to be reminded periodically. Learning must be recursive, both to remind us of what we have forgotten and because with each revisit we bring added maturity and wisdom. Other follow-up lessons explore and expand upon how to use each of these discrete skills: identifying types of text structures, using text features, scanning, skimming, and summarizing.

Determining Importance with Online Resources

To demonstrate to my fourth-grade students the importance of sifting and sorting information, I have them visit Sky View Café, an online planetarium.[9] As the introduction to Sky View Café notes, you can use the interactive features to see the night sky as it appears over your hometown and view the constellations, planets, moons of Jupiter and Saturn, and a multitude of deep sky objects 4.0 magnitude or brighter. First I have students click on the Find button and enter our location. The sky as it appears above Lansdowne, Maryland, is displayed. Students see the hundreds of stars and handful of planets visible that night with the unaided eye or an amateur telescope. Next I have them click in the box to show all the constellations. Finally, I have students click on Show Names and choose Show All Deep Sky Objects. The nighttime sky is now so crowded with objects that it is impossible to tell where one begins and another ends.

"Determining what is important," I tell my fourth graders, "depends on your purpose for finding the information. If you need information about constellations as they appear in the nighttime sky above Lansdowne, then the information about deep sky objects is not only extraneous but also confusing. In fact, we have to sift out the information about deep sky objects in order to even see the constellations. On the other hand, if we need information about the deep sky objects, then we need to sift out the information about constellations and planets. Knowing what information you need helps you determine what is important."

Sifting information is particularly important when you are using online resources because there is so much information available online that it is easy to be overwhelmed. Today we're going to begin an online research model, "Oh Starry Night," where we will learn how our position in space affects the way we see celestial bodies and how to determine importance when using online resources.[10] Online research models, based on Jamie McKenzie's work, provide a framework for students to learn how to gather, sift, sort, analyze, synthesize, and use information to solve real-world problems. "Oh Starry Night" asks students to create a sky map based on their observations of the nighttime sky and their research. In addition, they research the mythology associated with a constellation they select from those that can be seen as they stare out their bedroom windows. Finally, students are asked to research and think about why since time immemorial humankind has seen events in the sky as omens or harbingers of things to come.

The majority of resources students will be using for this research are written well above a fourth-grade reading level. Thus, to be successful students must be able to search effectively and efficiently by using keywords and Boolean operators; quickly discard information that does not meet their needs; scan the text structure; skim the topic sentences; utilize text features, including text features like buttons and hyperlinks that are unique to online resources; summarize the information; and use technology as an aid in summarizing and annotating their research.

Today's mini-lesson will focus on utilizing online text features to determine importance; the other skills have already been addressed in previous lessons. To demonstrate how to use online text features, I have students click on the next resource in "Oh Starry Night," Discovery School's "Sky Watch."[11] The opening paragraph begins, "What do you see when you look up at the night sky? A jumbled mass of stars?" I tell my fourth graders, "I don't know about you, but what I see when I look at this page is a jumbled mass of texts and graphics." There are twelve buttons on the left. Underneath the buttons is an empty box that I first thought must be a search box, but it turns out to be how you sign up for a newsletter. A photo of star clusters is next to the text. Nothing is underlined to indicate that it is a hyperlink. There are different colors used for some of the text, and when I pass the mouse over it, it turns from a cursor to a hand, so I know that some of the colored text is hyperlinked. There are phrases that look like they may be subheadings because they are in all capital letters, but they are not in a different color so I am not sure if they are hyperlinks. "To determine importance," I tell them, "first I have to be able to use the online text features to find the information."

Assuming that children know how to use technology effectively and efficiently just because they are more tech savvy than many adults is a mistake. Children must be shown how to use online text features to find information and determine importance. I model how to use online text features as students take notes. Children were amazed that websites like Discovery School have a search box and even more astonished and confused when it did not work like the search engines, such as Yahooligans, they are accustomed to using. Other children were surprised that sometimes colored text indicates a hyperlink. Many did not realize that when the cursor turns into a hand that means that you click on the link; students assumed that the hand meant you could move the text just like you can move objects in Kid Pix and other drawing programs with the hand. Without knowing how to access hyperlinks that were not underlined, students would have been unable to use the subheadings "How to See the Stars" and "Sky Stories," which they need to complete their research. In addition, they would have been unable to determine if the subheadings helped them determine importance.

Over two decades of research show that the same strategies good readers use to locate the main ideas or themes can be taught to less-than-proficient readers; however, showing children where to look is only the first step. The next step is showing children how to sift, sort, analyze, and use in meaningful ways the big ideas uncovered in their reading if they are to comprehend not only the texts they read but also the real world. The ability to determine importance by identifying the main ideas or themes is critical to comprehension; it is equally important to reading "men and nations."

NOTES

1. I have frequently thought that my job would be much easier if highlighters came with usage instructions!

2. Their findings are not at all surprising given how comprehension is measured. Comprehension tests measure the reader's ability to choose from a set of given responses the one that best represents the main idea in nonfiction or theme in fiction.

3. A hierarchy implies that certain strategies are more important, at the pinnacle, than others. Each of the strategies I present is critical to developing comprehension and engagement. All are utilized by proficient readers at different points in the meaning-making process. The trick, of course, is to show students how and when to use each strategy as they construct knowledge.

4. Why not simply give students a graphic organizer containing all of the story elements? If I give them a graphic organizer for each task, they use it as both a crutch and a cue to what they should be thinking and doing. My goal is to create independent readers who are able to think critically and strategically.

5. I would love to continue thinking aloud, but the amount of squirming going on tells me that it is past time for students to share. Even though students are not passive listeners as I think out loud (they are actively engaged in taking notes), first graders, particularly at the end of the day on a Friday afternoon, have a short attention span.

6. A KWL chart is an organizer students use to recall what they Know, to think about what they Want to learn, and to list what they Learned.

7. It is important to make the distinction that themes are what we, the readers, learn, not what the character learns—for at least two major reasons. First, by stating that themes are what we the readers learn, we immediately remove the lessons from the realm of fiction and transfer these big ideas to our very real world. Second, further in their studies, children encounter limited protagonists whose tragic flaws are their inability to learn from their experiences and actions.

8. I am always shocked by the number of children and adults who do not use the Table of Contents or the Index to quickly locate the information they need.

9. Find the Sky View Café at http://www.skyviewcafe.com/skyview.php.

10. "Oh Starry Night" and other online research models are available at http://www.bcps.org/offices/lis/models/index.html. Simply click on the grade level and content area you want to view.

11. Find "Sky Watch" at http://school.discovery.com/schooladventures/skywatch/index.html. The Discovery School website is a truly outstanding online resource and much better organized than most. The problem is not how the site is organized, although some consistency about the appearance of hyperlinks would be helpful, but that students must be taught how to use online text features.

8

Inferring
and
Predicting

*The power to guess the unseen
from the seen, to trace the implications
of things, to judge the whole piece by the
pattern, the condition of feeling life in
general so completely that you are well
on your way to knowing any particular
corner of it—this cluster of gifts may
almost be said to constitute experience.*

Henry James

*T*he "power to guess the unseen from the seen" is the ability to make inferences. It is also the foundation for comprehending the myriad of implied understandings that underlie writing in every discipline, genre, and form. Singer (1988) defines inferring as the ability to make connections, perceive possible relationships, and see links between textual units like sentences, paragraphs, and chapters or sections. He adds that the ability to infer is so important that it is a "cornerstone of language processing." Inferring is not only the cornerstone of language processing but also the cornerstone of communication in all its forms: writing, speech, sign language, and the visual and electronic media of film, television, graphs, photos, illustrations, multimedia presentations, and the World Wide Web. Inferring and its forward-looking twin, predicting, are critical to comprehension of every form of communication but equally vital for interpreting life. The child who cannot infer from and make predictions based on the body language of his or her parents, teachers, and peers becomes socially maladjusted and is at risk for both academic and social failure. More seriously, children who cannot interpret the world around them, especially clues that signal danger, are at risk for much more than academic failure. Fortunately, the vast majority of children have few problems judging "the whole piece from the pattern." The large gap apparent in research study after study between proficient readers' abilities to make inferences and the inability of poor, or less skilled, readers is not a gap in the life skill of inferring meaning (Winne, Graham, and Prock 1993). Rather, it is a gap in the ability to make text-based inferences.

Inferring

Show the average or below-average kindergarten student a picture of a little boy crying while holding a teddy bear missing an arm and he or she will be able to tell you what they infer: the little boy is sad because his favorite teddy is torn. Add a sad-looking puppy, and every child will be able to infer that the puppy chewed the teddy. Increase the level of abstraction by substituting a crying smiley face and a symbol representing a broken toy, and children will still be able to infer what happened: the smiley face is feeling very sad (or as sad as a smiley face can feel!) because its toy is broken. The problem is not inferring from abstract representations; the problem is inferring from text. There are specific text-based reasons that explain the discrepancy between children's ability to infer in real life or from pictures and their ability to transfer that skill to reading. Such children have problems making the following:[1]

Connections between the text and personal experiences, including knowledge of other texts and the world

Rich, detailed visualizations

Self-generated questions

Anaphoric inferences (the ability to infer the antecedent of a pronoun clause; the ability to identify the deliberate repetition of a word or phrase at the beginning of several successive verses, clauses, or paragraphs)

Vocabulary inferences

Thematic inferences

Text structure and unit inferences

Inferences based on academic, procedural, or prior knowledge

Ways to address the first three problems are covered in depth in earlier chapters, but it bears repeating that children who do not connect to, visualize from, and ask questions of the text are not actively engaged in making meaning. As disengaged readers, they have great difficulty transferring their ability to make inferences in the real world to the text because they do not perceive the text as its own world filled with complex and interesting characters, just like the people they know in their everyday life. They cannot "read" the actions of the text's characters because they perceive them as at best one-dimensional figures, cardboard cutouts without feelings and emotions. In nonfiction, these readers' lack of knowledge about how to connect, visualize, and question results in their inability to use prior knowledge to fill in the gaps in the text; to visualize complex processes, like mitosis; and to ask questions and seek answers. Modeling how to make connections, create visualizations, and ask questions are essential first steps in teaching children how to infer.

Readers who have difficulty with the fourth problem, following *anaphoric inferences*, are those who cannot readily track antecedents. Skilled readers, on the other hand, use anaphoric inferences to identify the antecedent of pronouns or noun clauses. For example, in the second sentence of the previous paragraph the proficient reader would easily trace backward the referent of "they" to "disengaged readers." Because "they" appears three times in the second sentence, the ability to infer its antecedent is critical to understanding it. Many readers have little difficulty understanding a reference when its antecedent is in the same sentence, but when the reference extends to other sentences, as it does in the paragraph above, or even to other paragraphs, less skilled readers become lost. Research shows that "one critical difference between skilled and less skilled readers is their ability to make inferences that complete cohesion gaps, particularly those involving pronominal reference. Skilled readers are more likely to resolve anaphors, especially when referent is distant" (Oakhill and Yuill 1986; Yuill and Oakhill 1988). McNamara and O'Reilly, citing Oakhill and Yuill (1986), note that comprehension of anaphors is more challenging in text than in conversations

> because there is little shared context in the former. In contrast, there is a wealth of contextual information available to the speakers in face to face conversations. Anaphor resolution difficulties are particularly problematic for younger and less skilled readers. This difficulty persists even when there is a gender cue and when the clause containing the referent is available to the reader. (2004, 11)

The implied subjects of noun clauses and imperative sentences pose additional problems for even skilled readers.

Vocabulary inferences present challenges for children less skilled in using context clues. Even children with robust vocabularies encounter unfamiliar words, particularly in content area reading. Stopping to look up the definition of every unknown word they encounter actually impedes comprehension, as several of my students discovered during their discussions of Jean Craighead George's books. Using context clues or the strategy of "reading on" helps students not only resolve gaps in their word knowledge but also build a rich vocabulary. Just as learning occurs more effectively in context, so too does vocabulary development. Words learned in context have deeper meaning for children because, not only is the definition provided by clues children have to think about, but also the word is used in context.

Difficulties making *thematic inferences* are generally related to problems in determining importance. Children cannot infer from the main idea or theme if they cannot find it in the sea of surrounding, supporting details. To overcome children's difficulties locating the main idea or theme, teachers and librarians must provide explicit instruction in determining importance. Effective comprehension strategy instruction is explicit; the instructor tells readers why and when they should use strategies, what strategies to use, and how to apply them. Then the instructor shows children how to use the strategy through modeling, gives guided practice, and provides ample time for independent application. Explicitly teaching children how to sift and sort information, as well as showing them how to think about what the texts show rather than tell, usually resolves difficulties in making thematic inferences.

Unable to recognize—particularly in poorly written texts—that two things are being compared and contrasted, less skilled readers see the contradictory information and become confused. In the absence of signal or semantic clues (or of knowledge of how signal words function), children are unable to make *text structure inferences*—particularly if, as is usually the case, the comparison and contrast occur over several paragraphs. The same is true for cause and effect, persuasive, sequential, and enumerative essays as well as narratives that jump back and forth in time or are disjointed. Modeling how to impose structure on poorly written texts and utilize text structures in well-written texts is a necessary precursor to teaching children how to infer.

All of us who have experienced frustration and confusion as we tried to program a DVD recorder or assemble modular furniture can appreciate problems involved with making *procedural inferences*. Children and adults who are unfamiliar with the tasks of assembling or programming cannot infer what they do not even know is missing; they are unable to bridge gaps in the directions because of their lack of experience. Only repeated exposure to the text (think how many times you refer back to the text when trying to assemble an object for the first time) combined with hands-on experimentation allows the reader to bridge the gap.

Academic inferences are also called *domain-* or *content-specific inferences*. Gaps in or lack of familiarity with specific content knowledge accounts for many of the difficulties students have inferring, particularly from nonfiction trade books and textbooks. In chapter 6 I modeled difficulties I had understanding a Cortese article on question-answer relationship strategies. At least in Cortese's article I had considerable schema to help me; put a physics textbook in front of me and you will really see someone struggling to make meaning. Because I lack the academic knowledge of physics that would help me comprehend, my energies are focused on the literal comprehension of the text. As a result, I have no energy left to divert to trying to infer. Expecting children to be able to infer during their first exposure to unfamiliar content is inviting failure. Only through repeated exposure and additional research can children build the knowledge base they need to infer effectively.

Teachers have long known that gaps in prior knowledge account for many of the difficulties in comprehension low-income students experience; unfortunately, the solution to the problem is not as simple as supplying the missing information. Children who are unable to infer from text experiences are just as unlikely to infer from your summary of the missing experience. Providing children with rich, diverse learning experiences through field trips (virtual and real) hands-on experimentation, role playing, readers' theater, assemblies, and access to complex, multifaceted, and multicultural texts will help to address gaps in their schema. Helping children make connections between their experiences and the experiences depicted in texts is also essential to helping them bridge the gap. For example, the majority of my children have never attended a summer camp, but many have been camping or at the very least have spent the night at a friend's house. They can use such experiences to help understand, for example, Ralph's amazing escapades in *Runaway Ralph* or Winnie's adventures in *Truly Winnie*.

In *7 Keys to Comprehension: How to Help Your Kids Read It and Get It!* Chryse Hutchins tells of a former fifth-grade teacher who told the young Chryse that inferring was "reading between the lines" (Zimmermann and

Hutchins 2003, 97). Hutchins recounts looking in the white spaces between the lines and never once finding an inference! Now, she tells her students that

> meaning is found between their ears, not between the lines. Inferring involves forming a best guess about what the "evidence" (words, sentences, and paragraphs) means; speculating about what's to come; and then drawing conclusions about what was read to deepen the meaning of the literal words on the page. (2003, 97)

Predicting

Predicting is inferring plus; the plus is an educated guess about what will happen next based on inferences made after thinking about the title, cover illustration, author, genre, text, text features and structures, pictures, and other illustrations as well as events and information. If inferring is using clues in the text to state explicitly what is happening now or what happened in the past, then predicting is using what happened now to foretell what will happen next. Much has been made about inferences being open-ended while predictions are confirmed or denied by events later in the text; however, inferences too must be confirmed or denied by the text. For example, if I infer from events in *Arthur's Valentine* that Arthur is too sick to go to school, but I later realize that he was embarrassed because his friends kept teasing him about his secret admirer, then I have correctly revised my inference. It is true that inferences may not be confirmed or denied by the end of the text, but the same is true of predictions. Proficient readers make predictions and inferences as they read; then they confirm or revise both based on events in the text and their deepening understanding. Clearly communicating to your students that good readers constantly revise predictions is important for two reasons. First, it conveys that reading is a dynamic, ongoing process; as new information is processed, understanding is refined. Second, children who make a prediction only to find that their prediction is refuted by what happens next become hesitant to make new predictions unless they realize or are shown that good readers constantly revise their predictions. Predicting is not like taking a test, I tell my students. There are no right or wrong answers, just good thinking about what may happen next.

Modeling Inferring and Predicting

One of my favorite books to use to introduce inferring and predicting to my kindergarteners is *Deep in the Forest* by Brinton Turkle. Turkle's wordless picture book tells the tale of what happens when baby bear surreptitiously visits the home of Goldilocks while her family is on a walk through the woods to allow time for their porridge to cool. Children's familiarity with *Goldilocks and the Three Bears* helps them make inferences and predictions in Turkle's reversal of one of their favorite fairy tales.

I begin by defining inferring and predicting with picture cards. I hold up a picture card I created using Microsoft's online clip art gallery; the card depicts a little boy crying and holding his scraped knee. I ask children to infer, or think about, what is happening based on the clues in the picture. Students have no trouble inferring that the little boy is crying because he fell and hurt his knee, and they are easily able to point to the clues in the picture that support their inference. Children immediately want to extrapolate about what happened to make the little boy fall, but I point out that one big difference between an inference and a guess is that an inference is based on clues.[2] I say, "So far, we do not have any clues to suggest how he fell."

Next I hold up a picture card showing the same picture with the addition of a bike lying on its side. "Who can infer what happened to the little boy? Remember, inferring is thinking about and explaining what happened based on the clues." Children are again easily able to infer that the boy is sad because he fell off the bike and hurt his knee. When asked for the supporting evidence or clues they used, children point to the bike, the tears, and the scraped knee. One child even infers that the boy may have fallen because he was riding his bike for the first time without its training wheels, a detail I hadn't noticed when I chose the picture.

I now hold up a succession of picture cards showing a child moaning and holding his stomach with an empty bag of cookies next to him; a little girl crying and pointing at a tree where a kite is stuck in the branches; and a child beaming as an adult hands her a paper with an A+ at the top. Children are again easily able to infer what is happening now in the pictures and what had happened in the immediate past: the little boy ate too many cookies and has a bellyache; the little girl flew her kite too close to a tree and is sad because now it is stuck, or the wind blew it into the tree; and the girl who received an A+ is very happy because she studied hard and got a "really, really good grade."

"Next," I tell them, "we're going to look at the same pictures and predict what will happen next. Predicting, like inferring, means thinking about and explaining based on clues in the text, but when you predict you say what will probably happen next. To predict, think about what usually happens to you, your family, friends, and characters in other books in the same situation." I hold up the picture card that shows the little boy crying and holding his scraped knee. "Based on your experiences and the clues in the picture, predict what you think will happen next." One child predicts that "he will go home and get his knee cleaned with that bubbly stuff, and then his mommy will put a Band-Aid on his knee." As evidence to support her prediction, she points out that the little boy has to go home because there is no house in the picture and that her mom always cleans her cuts and puts on a Band-Aid. Other children quickly give a thumbs-up in agreement. A few children want to elaborate on what kind of bandage the mom puts on the scrape; to head off a spirited discussion about which cartoon character they want on their bandages, I quickly show the next picture card: the little boy with the scrape and the bike in the background. Their predictions about what will happen next are more thoughtful and reflective. Although they are sure that the little boy will still go home for treatment, they are about equally divided over if and when he will ride his bike again. Some predict that he will, but first he will have the training wheels put back on the bike. Others know from experience that you have to fall many times before you learn how to ride a bike. Children continue to think about and predict for the remaining picture cards.

"Wow," I tell them, "you are doing such a great job inferring and predicting that I think you are ready to infer and to predict with one of my favorite wordless picture books, *Deep in the Forest*. Because there are no words, we'll have to do a lot of thinking, inferring, and predicting. Watch what I do and say for the first few pages, then maybe you'll help me make a list that we can use when it's your turn." I turn to the first page, which depicts a baby bear creeping ever closer to the open door of a log cabin situated, I infer from the title, deep in the woods. Students watch as I carefully observe the picture and then infer that the cabin is probably empty because there is no one in the window and no smoke coming from the chimney. I predict that the baby bear will probably go into the log cabin because the door is open and the cabin looks empty. I turn the page and confirm that my prediction was right; the baby bear is peering around the cabin door. I point out that "sometimes my predictions do not come true and that's okay; the important thing is that I'm thinking about the story and using the clues the author gave me."

Next I look carefully at the double-spread illustration. "I see three bowls and a pitcher on the table, three chairs, and three beds in the next room. I can infer that three people probably live in the cabin, but they are not home right now. One bed is clearly bigger than the next one, which in turn is bigger than the bed next to it. Hmmm," I say, "I wonder if the same is true of the chairs and the bowls." I look back and notice that both the chairs and the bowls go from largest to smallest. "Except that it's a bear looking through the door, this book is starting to remind me of another story. If I'm right about the connection, then I predict that next the bear will eat porridge from the bowls." I turn the page and observe that the bear has its front paws up on the bench and is licking its lips. "I bet we can all infer what the bear is feeling and thinking." Children eagerly share that they infer that the bear is feeling hungry and is thinking about eating what is in the bowls. They just as eagerly predict that the bear will discover that one bowl is too hot, one is too cold, and the other bowl will be just right. We laugh when I turn the page and we see the bear holding what we infer to be his burnt paw after tasting the porridge in the big bowl; turning his nose up at what we infer to be the cold porridge in the medium-sized bowl; and eagerly licking every single drop from the small bowl.

Before we read the rest of the book, I ask children to share what inferring and predicting looks and sounds like:

"You make connections with what you know."

"Yeah, and you make connections to stories you know."

"You think about the clues in the pictures."

"You use the clues to think about what's happening now and what's going to happen next."

"Predicting is when you think about what happens next."

"When you infer, you think about what is happening now."

"You look at the pictures carefully."

"Sometimes, you go back and look at the pictures again."

When asked how they think inferring and predicting will help them become better readers, children responded "that all that thinking just has to help you" and that "predicting will help you guess at words you don't know," to mention just a few of their insights. We continue to practice inferring and predicting as I finish sharing Turkle's picture book. Next, children practice inferring and predicting with predictable texts like *If You Give a Pig a Pancake* by Laura Numeroff, *Jillian Jiggs* by Phoebe Gilman, the many versions of *I Know an Old Lady Who Swallowed a Fly*, and Bill Martin's *Brown Bear, Brown Bear, What Do You See?*

Teaching about Anaphoric and Vocabulary Inferences

It's March, Women's History Month, and fourth graders are just finishing their study of Native American cultures, so an article about Sacagawea (*KIDS Discover*, January 2002) seems like the perfect vehicle to teach students to trace anaphors back to their antecedents and use context clues to infer the meaning of unfamiliar words. These fourth graders already have experience inferring and predicting; they have been using the two strategies extensively as they make meaning from the many resources they consulted about Native Americans. In addition, the majority of students, except for the new transfers, have been taught how to use the two strategies in second and third grades.[3] Prior to students' arrival, I have gathered a class set of the magazine, cut translucent light blue report covers in half for use by students as overlays, and prepared a transparency of the passage to use for modeling.[4]

After children check their books in and out, they sit at the tables where we will be working today. I begin by explaining that today I will be modeling two types of inferences skilled readers make: anaphoric and vocabulary. Then I describe anaphoric inferences—inferring the antecedent of pronouns or noun clauses. Students are familiar with pronouns and noun clauses but aren't quite sure what an antecedent is, so I promptly define it for them. I also explain why writers use anaphors: to avoid boring repetitions. "Today," I tell them, "I'm going to model how good readers use visualizing and inferring to trace the anaphor's antecedent and the context clues for unfamiliar words." Then I read and think aloud about the passage displayed on the overhead:

> By the fall of 1804, Sacagawea was expecting her first child. But that didn't prevent Charbonneau, a wanderer by nature, from asking Lewis and Clark if they would hire him as an interpreter. He knew Hidatsa and the sign language common among the river tribes. Lewis and Clark enlisted him

right away. When they found out he was married to a Shoshone, they encouraged him to bring her along. They had heard that the Shoshone had fine horses, which they would need later. They figured the presence of Sacagawea would make the Shoshone more open to negotiations. Also, Indians they encountered would view them as peaceful since war parties never included women. (*KIDS Discover*, January 2002, 8)

"Finding the antecedent for the first pronoun is easy. The 'her' in the first sentence has to refer back to Sacagawea; to help me visualize the connection, I am going to draw an arrow from 'her' back to its referent, 'Sacagawea.' Finding the antecedent for 'him' in the second sentence is a little more difficult because there are so many words separating 'him' from its referent, Charbonneau, but I know he has to be the antecedent because he asked Lewis and Clark to hire him. I am going to draw an arrow to connect 'him' to 'Charbonneau.' Now, good readers do not actually draw the arrow; they just visualize it, but I find that drawing the arrow helps when students are first learning how to use anaphoric inferences."

I continue, tracing the "he" in the third sentence and the "him" in the fourth sentence back to "Charbonneau." Then I say, "Imagine how boring this passage would be if the author kept repeating 'Charbonneau.' Now, imagine how confused I would be right now if I didn't know who all of these pronouns were referring to." Students help me draw arrows to show the antecedents of the ten remaining pronouns in the paragraph.

My next task is to show students how to use context clues to unlock the meaning of unfamiliar words. I circle the word *interpreter* in the second sentence and say, "If I didn't know what 'interpreter' meant I could look for context clues." I read the next sentence, "He knew Hidatsa and the sign language common among the river tribes," and think aloud "an interpreter must be someone who knows Hidatsa, the language of the tribe that kidnapped Sacagawea when she was a child, and other languages. From the context clues, I infer that an interpreter is someone who knows other languages." I draw a circle around "knew Hidatsa and the sign language common among the river tribes" and draw a two-way arrow connecting the two circles.[5] I think aloud, use context clues, and infer the meaning for *enlisted* and *encountered*.

After we discuss what making anaphoric and vocabulary inferences looks and sounds like and how it helps us become better readers, students break into partners and choose a portion of the text to analyze. They place the blue transparency over the text so that they can link pronouns to their antecedents. They draw connecting arrows on the overlay and reason aloud to each other how they inferred the antecedent and how using context clues helped them learn new words. In the next lesson, they will model their thinking for the rest of the class.

Making these inferences helps students not only understand the text but also acquire new knowledge, be it vocabulary or content knowledge or simply new general background knowledge, like the fact that the wild artichokes Sacagawea gathered were edible. Much of the information we learn from texts is never stated explicitly. Teaching children how to infer and predict from elements in the text, combined with their background knowledge of how the world, and texts, work, enables them to become independent, successful makers of meaning.

NOTES

1. This list of text-based problems is a synthesis and distillation of various sources, including Harvey and Goudvis (2000), Miller (2002), and my experiences teaching; additionally, Pretorius (2000) contains an excellent overview and analysis of how the inability to make vocabulary, anaphoric, and academic inferences impedes tertiary students at the University of South Africa.
2. One child in this class attributes everything that happens to her imaginary horse. If she is running in the hall, it's because of the horse. If she's unable to sit still that day, a fairly frequent occurrence, it's because of the horse. As soon as her hand went up in the air, I just knew that she was going to attribute the boy's fall to her horse. Asking children to point to or cite the clues that support their inferences helps eliminate overly imaginative responses.
3. The 2004/5 school year is our third year of full implementation of strategy instruction.
4. I use light blue because it reduces the glare from glossy magazine pages and may (the jury is still out) help children whose reading disabilities are at least partially related to visual difficulties. I use report covers because they are so much cheaper than overhead transparencies.
5. I use a different-colored transparency marker to make it easier to differentiate between the two types of inferences. You could also use two transparencies and remove the first after you finish modeling anaphoric inferences.

9

Analyzing and Synthesizing

*Books
are the ships
which pass through
the vast sea
of time.*

Francis Bacon

*W*riting in *Library Media Connection*, R. J. Todd states,

> The hallmark of a school library in the 21st century is not its collections, its systems, its technology, its staffing, its buildings, but its actions and evidences that show that it makes a real difference to student learning, that it contributes in tangible and significant ways to the development of human understanding, meaning making, and constructing knowledge. (2003, 12)

The comprehension strategies discussed in the previous chapters aid the growth of human understanding and the ability to make meaning, but it is the final two strategies, analyzing and synthesizing, that build new knowledge. Although these two strategies work in tandem, they represent diametrically different processes: *analysis* is the separation of something into its component parts; *synthesis* is the assembly of parts into a new whole.

Analysis is critical to developing understanding and making meaning in every discipline. Writers, readers, and thinkers analyze problems, processes, events, and ideas by breaking each into its smallest unit. Synthesis, on the other hand, is the integration of two or more preexisting elements that results in a new creation: a molecule, an art form, or a philosophical system. Synthesis is the ultimate goal of learning, for it is through synthesis that new knowledge is created. Representing the epitome of human thought, it is the last of the comprehension strategies to be taught. "At its best, synthesizing involves merging new information with existing knowledge to create an original idea, see a new perspective, or form a new line of thinking to achieve insight" (Harvey and Goudvis 2000, 143).

As you read the previous paragraph, synthesis was occurring at a phenomenal rate within your body. Biochemists who study the synthesis of the hundreds of thousands of proteins, lipids, carbohydrates, and nucleic acids produced each day from precursors in the human body know that synthesis does not happen randomly. In nature, synthesis occurs slowly or not at all in the absence of a catalyst and specific precursors. In learning, synthesis happens rarely by chance but often through careful curriculum design. Here are some important catalysts for synthesis in learning:

- Juxtapositions of genres, images, data, texts, and disciplines
- Thought-provoking quotes, images, or data
- Essential questions
- Real-world problems
- Authentic assessments
- Multiple knowledge sources

"The human mind is a meaning-making machine," I tell my students. Juxtapose, put side by side, data from twenty years ago with data from today, and the mind starts to forge connections and impute trends. Juxtaposing quotations with text, data, or images also provokes thought and leads to insight. When you put two unlike things together, the mind immediately starts to make connections between them. For example, place a copy of one of the earliest photos ever taken with this chapter's opening epigraph from Bacon and immediately students begin to build bridges between the two. Proficient thinkers go beyond the mind's automatic processing to the next level and begin to ask questions, visualize, and determine importance. McKenzie theorizes that sharply contrasting images create dissonance. "The sharper the contrast, the greater the dissonance. We can feel the vibration, the conflict, the discomfort. We are thrown off balance. Our minds are intrigued, our curiosities awakened. We want to resolve the dissonance, bring things back into harmony or resonance" (2000, 35–36). In the process of resolving the dissonance by analyzing the disparate pieces, insight and synthesis are achieved.

Mike Eisenberg (1998) writes that "synthesis is the result, the output part of the information process." It takes place in research when children are challenged to employ thoughtful reading, analysis, and evaluation of information to create answers, not just find them. Research that requires students to make authentic choices and solve real problems serves as a potent catalyst for both analysis and synthesis. For example, my fifth-grade students are challenged to design a safe playground in the online research model "Geoplayground."[1] To be successful, they must

> Collaborate with group members. Each member of the group is responsible for researching and designing a different type of playground apparatus.

> Gather and analyze information about the number and types of injuries children sustain each year on playground equipment.

> Research plans for and examples of safe playgrounds.

> Synthesize their research and knowledge of playgrounds, geometry, and physics to design the blueprint for a safe playground. Each person in the group is responsible for analyzing the safe fall zone, the height of and distance from other equipment. For example, the person who researches swings calculates the fall zone; the maximum and minimum heights of the swing; and the distance the swing must be from the slides, seesaws, and other climbing equipment.

> Use their knowledge of geometric forms to build a model of the sturdiest and safest playground equipment they can construct.

Children employ analysis and synthesis throughout the process of solving this very real-world problem; each child has been or knows someone who has been injured, sometimes seriously, on the playground.

Essential questions like "How can we use our knowledge of physics and geometry to create a safer playground?" fuel the research process; these open-ended, overarching questions require students to analyze and synthesize information. There are no pat answers to an essential question; instead,

> essential questions require that students spend time pondering the importance and meaning of information. Most essential questions are interdisciplinary in nature. They cut across the lines created by schools and scholars to mark the terrain of departments and disciplines. Essential

questions probe the deepest issues confronting us . . . complex and baffling matters which elude simple answers: Life—Death—Marriage—Identity—Purpose—Betrayal—Honor—Integrity—Courage—Temptation—Faith—Leadership—Addiction—Invention—Inspiration.

(McKenzie 2001, 5)

The child who asks "How can a mother just up and leave her children?" after reading Patricia MacLachlan's *Journey* is asking an essential question. The online research model that asks "How can the power of 'one' affect the natural relationships in the Chesapeake Bay?" is posing an essential question. To answer the essential question, students must analyze and synthesize information from multiple sources. In addition, the model the students build is not only a synthesis of what they have learned but also an authentic assessment.

Juxtaposing two or more information resources results in analysis and synthesis because no two sources have exactly the same information. Emphasis is given to one idea by this author and to another by the second author. Some sources are detail rich; others focus on imparting the main idea. In addition, the authors' biases and writing styles leave an indelible stamp on each work. In their efforts to reconcile the differences, children use analysis by breaking down the sources into their component parts, organizing the information and then comparing the similarities and differences.

To summarize the results of their analysis, children use synthesis. They combine parts of each source to create something new and unique: their summaries. Synthesis need not result in the creation of a new philosophy, like Hegelianism, or a movement, like postmodernism; the results of synthesis can be and usually are as simple as a poster illustrating ways children at Lansdowne can save the Chesapeake Bay, tans arranged to form a new tangram character, or a picture book students write to explain to younger children what happens when they are hurt or sick.

Modeling Analyzing and Synthesizing

My second graders have checked out new library books, gathered their tools for thinking, and examined the definitions of analysis and synthesis displayed on our thinking board. They are excited that today we will be learning about not one but two strategies. I begin with an analogy to help them visualize the abstract concepts of analysis and synthesis. "Analysis is like taking a completed puzzle apart and examining every piece. You look at how the pieces fit together and begin to notice patterns. Next you sort the different pieces; maybe you put all the corner pieces in one pile and all the pieces that are not corners, but have outside edges, into another pile.

"On the other hand, synthesis is *not*," I shake my head emphatically, "like putting that same puzzle back together again. When you synthesize, you take parts from two or more different things and put them together so that they fit perfectly into something entirely new. It would be like trying to perfectly fit together puzzle pieces from different puzzles. To make the pieces fit you would need to take a little bit off of one piece and maybe add or take even more off the second piece. You would have to get it just right or there would be a gap between the two pieces; they wouldn't fit together perfectly. It sounds really hard, doesn't it?" Children nod their heads. "It is hard. It requires a lot of deep thinking and using all the strategies we have learned, but I know what great thinkers you are, so I know that everyone will be able to analyze and synthesize by the end of the period."

I look around and wait to hear the "No, that's too hard, Ms. Grimes," but no one makes so much as a peep in protest. By the end of the year, children no longer doubt me when I make audacious claims. They have faith in themselves and confidence in their abilities to think critically and creatively.

"Today, we are going to analyze *Grandfather Tang's Story*, a tale told with tangrams by a grandfather and his granddaughter. As I'm sure you remember, a tangram is a Chinese puzzle made from a square cut into five triangles, a square, and a rhomboid.[2] The Chinese call a tangram the seven pieces of cleverness because you need to be very clever to create a tangram character. You also need to be able to analyze and sort the seven pieces by thinking about the different properties of each shape."

I model analysis by thinking about the characteristics of each shape, like the number of sides and angles, as I cut it from the square I have prepared. Then I think aloud about and group the different pieces. "If I put two triangles together, then I have a square, but if I put them together another way I have a rhomboid." I continue to sort by flipping, rotating, and sliding the various tangram pieces. I talk about looking at every angle of the problem, a joke my students find hilarious—but then it doesn't take much to amuse second graders.

Next I give them their job: to observe and record what analysis looks and sounds like when applied to a story in preparation for when it's their turn to analyze the story and the tangrams. Children take notes as I analyze the various story elements, especially the tangram characters Grandfather creates of the two fox fairies, Chou and Wu Ling, who can magically transform themselves into any creature. I compare and contrast the characters just as I did the tangram pieces. Then the children listen as I put the pieces back together by summarizing the beginning and middle of the story: "Chou and Wu Ling are the best of friends, but like many friends sometimes there is rivalry, so when Wu Ling changes into a rabbit, Chou changes into a dog who 'not only looked like a dog, but he felt like a dog and acted like a dog.' Dogs, of course, love to chase rabbits, and that is exactly what Chou proceeds to do, so Wu Ling changes into a squirrel so he can climb a tree and escape. The friends keep trying to outdo each other until suddenly, not only is their friendship in danger, but so are they."

I invite children to share what analyzing looks and sounds like. One thing they notice quickly is how similar analysis is to determining importance:

"For both, you look at the beginning, middle, and end."

"You also pay attention to what happens to the main character."

"For each, you think about what the story shows, not tells."

"When you analyze, though, you do more comparing and contrasting; you also look more closely at how the pieces fit together."

"When you determine importance, you look at everything, but only to see if it is important."

"It's like when you were looking at the tangram pieces; when you analyze you look at it from every angle."

"When you analyze, you take all of the pieces apart."

"When you analyze, you think about all of the characters, the many different settings, the plot structure, and the events," I add. Judging from their remarks, I know that students are now ready to analyze the remainder of the story with some guidance.

After we complete our analysis, we turn our attention to synthesis. "I chose *Grandfather Tang's Story* to introduce analysis and synthesis because I think the book *is* a synthesis. The author took her knowledge of tangrams and her knowledge of Chinese folktales and put them together to form a new creation, her story. Then she created another type of synthesis when she created the tangram characters. What different types of knowledge did she put together to make the tangram characters?" Children decide that she put together her knowledge of tangrams, including what she knew about shapes and how you can slide, flip, and rotate the pieces; information about how animals look and act, for example, that dogs chase rabbits; and her imagination.

"Now," I announce, "it's your turn to create a synthesis, a fusion of two or more different kinds of knowledge. You are going to create an original tangram character, not one you saw in the book because then it wouldn't be a new idea. You will need your imagination; your knowledge of how to slide, flip, and rotate tangram pieces; and what you know about the story to create a synthesis: a new tangram character that Wu Ling and Chou will meet in the sequel we will begin writing next week. Once you have created your character, you will mount it on a paper bag, like a puppet, so we can act out the sequel."

Together, we brainstorm characters the two fox fairies might meet in their next set of adventures. One child who loves the Aflac Insurance commercials immediately knows that he wants to create the duck; obviously, given the dangerous adventures the two have, they need insurance, he explains. Another child wants to create a snake, not only because he likes snakes but also because he thinks a snake will be easy to make from the tangram pieces. A group of children want the two fox fairies to travel back in time to the age of dinosaurs. They ask for permission to work together to create several kinds of dinosaurs and to write a sequel on their own. Still other children want to create bats, dragons, and "real fairies," like in Cinderella.

By the end of the period, the children have not only created a synthesis but also mounted it on a paper bag to use as a puppet in the sequels they are already planning on writing next week. In the next few weeks, we will talk about how writing is a type of synthesis and continue to hone our use of the comprehension strategies analyzing and synthesizing.

Using Juxtaposition to Induce Analysis and Synthesis

The easiest way to catalyze analysis and synthesis is through the juxtaposition of genres, images, data, texts, ideas, and disciplines, but the library media specialist and classroom teachers are not the only ones capable of creating these juxtapositions. Third-grade students who are studying the Chesapeake Bay will first gather data sets from the probes maintained by the Maryland Department of Natural Resources that constantly monitor key water quality indices, especially the dissolved oxygen (DO) concentration.[3] They know from their research at the MDNR website that, "since most aquatic organisms such as shellfish and other living resources require oxygen to survive, this is a very important measure of water quality. DO concentrations below 5 mg/l can stress organisms. DO levels of around 1 mg/l can result in fish kills." The data are available online, so it is easy for students to juxtapose DO data sets for 2003 and 2004 (figures 9-1 and 9-2). Because

FIGURE 9-1

Data Download: Chesapeake Bay, 2003

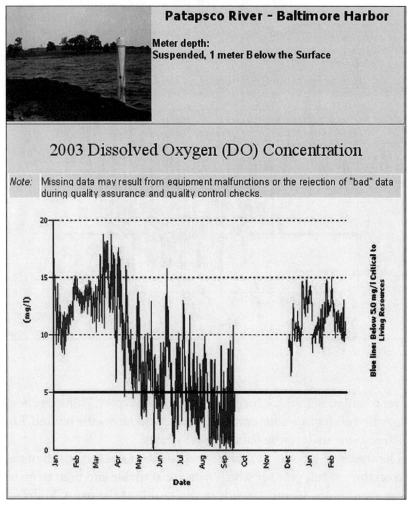

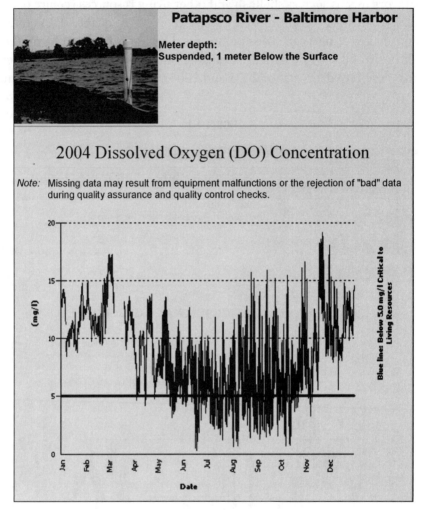

FIGURE 9-2

Data Download: Chesapeake Bay, 2004

Patapsco River - Baltimore Harbor

Meter depth:
Suspended, 1 meter Below the Surface

2004 Dissolved Oxygen (DO) Concentration

Note: Missing data may result from equipment malfunctions or the rejection of "bad" data during quality assurance and quality control checks.

data represented in graphic form are easier to interpret, children choose to display the results as a line graph. Even my student with limited English proficiency can analyze the data in these charts.

The students' job was to analyze the data to assess the health of the bay based on the last full year for which data are available and then to juxtapose the two data sets to identify trends in the health of the bay. Children were

Analyzing and Synthesizing

easily able to identify the months when DO concentrations fell below levels critical to living resources. They were also easily able to identify tentatively both trends in the health of the bay and the need for more information. After gathering additional information, particularly about the effects of pollutants and temperature changes on the underwater grasses that produce oxygen, they had no trouble synthesizing their research into posters suggesting ways that students at Lansdowne could save the bay. Their suggestions ranged from walking to baseball practice instead of having mom or dad drive them to reduce the amount of sulfur and nitrogen in the air to washing their hands in cold water to reduce the amount of energy used to heat water.

Using Writing to Catalyze Synthesis

Donald Graves has been quoted as saying that "writing is the ultimate act of synthesis" (Harvey and Goudvis 2000, 155). For my fifth-grade students, it will also be the authentic assessment of what they have learned about how body systems function in a healthy person and what happens within each system when a person is sick or injured. In order to answer the essential question "How does knowledge of how our body systems function empower us?"[4] students spent the previous three weeks researching the following questions:

What are the different parts of the body system? How does each part contribute to the job the whole system does?

How does the body system function?

Why is the system important to the body?

When does this body system function?

What is unique about this body system?

How does the system work to fight sickness and heal injuries?

Having gathered, organized, and analyzed the answers, students are ready to synthesize their results by writing a picture book that explains to young children what happens inside your body when you are sick or injured. The task is an authentic one because, not only are students asked to synthesize everything they have learned, but also their picture books have a real audience: sick or injured pediatric patients waiting in emergency rooms for treatment.

I tell my students, "Knowledge *is* power, especially when you are sick or hurt. A young child is terrified when he or she sees blood; when they know what blood is and how it moves around the body, they become less afraid. They are just as scared the first time they vomit. Knowing how and why we vomit gives young children control even when they can't control the vomiting or diarrhea. Your job is to synthesize what you know about body systems and translate it into language children can understand. You will also need to synthesize your knowledge to create illustrations to accompany and help explain the text."

As always, I am amazed by the results. When you give students a real audience and an authentic purpose for writing, you too will be amazed by what they can accomplish. One of my favorites was titled "There She Blows." It explained how and why we vomit by comparing vomiting to a volcanic eruption. Other students personified the various body systems by having, for example, Mr. Heart take you on a tour of the circulatory system and explaining what happens when you get a cut or bruise.

Synthesis needs a catalyst, whether it be to initiate the cascade of chemical reactions that occur in the human body or to create a new insight. Juxtaposing images, texts, and data is one way to catalyze synthesis. Engaging students in research tasks that require them to synthesize multiple sources to solve real-world problems is another important way to induce synthesis. But the most important catalyst is the person standing behind the circulation desk or in front of the classroom. Synthesis does not happen often by accident; instead, it happens when you design learning experiences that go beyond "read and report" to include thoughtful reading, analysis, evaluation, and synthesis of information to create answers, not just find them.

NOTES

1. To access this and other online research models referred to throughout this chapter, simply go to www.bcps.org/offices/lis/models/index.html and click on elementary, middle, or high school.

2. My children studied and manipulated tans earlier in the year as we prepared to celebrate the Chinese New Year. The online research model, which includes some truly wonderful sites that allow students to manipulate and learn about tans, is found at http://www.bcps.org/offices/lis.

3. When you want children to think like scientists, it is important that you give them access to the same tools used by scientists. The monitoring stations maintained by the Maryland Department of Natural Resources give students access to the same real-time and near-time data that scientists and policy-makers use to assess the health of the bay; see http://mddnr.chesapeakebay .net/eyesonthebay/index.cfm.

4. From the online research model "Dem Bones," available at http://www.bcps .org/offices/lis.

10

Transforming Our Libraries to Make Reading Our Business

"When I grow up," I tell her,
"I too will go to faraway places
and come home to live by the sea."

"That is all very well, little Alice,"
says my aunt,
"but there is a third thing
you must do."

"What is that?" I ask.

"You must do something to make
the world more beautiful."

Barbara Cooney,
Miss Rumphius

*D*ebbie Abilock (2004) compares "the remarkable young readers who are enthralled by the drama of stories, the details of a dinosaur's behavior, or the workings of a backhoe" to delicate alpine flowers that bloom only after years of protected growth. And she adds that, "in today's cold climate of flawed, 'scientifically based' practice, these alpine flowers are struggling to survive in an inhospitable landscape." She urges us to do everything in our power to protect and nurture these young readers who "tackle books dotted with multisyllabic words and navigate through trellised sentences that climb across many lines of text."

Not only must we protect and nurture these rare young readers, but we must also do more to propagate the same strategies that these proficient readers employ seemingly naturally. Like Miss Rumphius, who spreads beauty by seeding lupines in the story of the same name by Barbara Cooney, I hope to spread the use of comprehension strategies though the "fields and hillsides," "along the highways and down the lanes," and especially "around the school" and in the library. The same strategies that proficient readers utilize can and must be taught to every reader who seeks entrance through our doors.

Reading *is* our business; to ensure that we have customers, we need to begin with the five steps outlined below to transform our libraries:

Step 1

Transform Our Physical Environments to Encourage Discourse and Reflection

- Build a community of readers and thinkers begins by creating an inviting and comfortable environment designed to encourage browsing. Like Borders and Barnes & Noble, public and school libraries can offer activities, comfortable seating, and a café-like atmosphere where discussions about books take place. The harsh fluorescent lights common to so many libraries can be softened by the warmth of an occasional table lamp. Comfortable chairs and upholstered stools can be arranged strategically at the end of aisles or grouped together to provide a common area for book clubs to meet in comfort. Café tables can be placed in areas where readers gather to talk, skim, and browse. Data ports or wireless networks should be readily available, as should listening centers for audio books and music CDs.[1] In school libraries, it is wise to separate the instructional area from the area designated for browsing, either with empty space or with a few short bookcases between the two areas. Overheads are indispensable for displaying passages for intensive analysis. Bulletin boards, instead of housing cute seasonal displays, can showcase students' smart thinking. Large chart paper or poster board is helpful for recording the checklists students create about what each of the strategies looks and sounds like.

- Display new books prominently, along with books children want to recommend to other readers. In our library, students' written recommendations are showcased in inexpensive acrylic 4- by 6-inch L-frames placed next to the book. To encourage students to select a wider variety of reading materials, I frequently pull fiction, nonfiction, and periodicals on related topics for special displays. For example, I saw a dramatic increase in checkouts of both fiction and nonfiction titles when I temporarily housed all of my dog fiction stories with the newly arrived puppy care books. Despite intensive instruction and improved signage, many of my younger patrons still have trouble navigating the complexity of the Dewey decimal system. This becomes even more challenging when, as is the case in some public libraries, juvenile nonfiction is inter-filed with adult nonfiction. In addition, some of my "nonfiction-only" readers never wander into the fiction section, and some of my "fiction-only" readers rarely browse either the nonfiction or the many poetry and fairy/folktale titles our library contains. Juxtaposing poetry books like *Hoops* by Robert Burleigh or the many Matt Christopher fiction titles about basketball with how-to books encouraged many students to select books they might otherwise have never tried.[2]

Step 2

Teach Comprehension Strategies through Storytimes

- Begin a study group with fellow librarians, teachers, or parents. Read *7 Keys to Comprehension: How to Help Your Kids Read It and Get It!* (Zimmermann and Hutchins 2003); *Strategies That Work: Teaching Comprehension to Enhance Understanding* (Harvey and Goudvis 2000); and *Reading with Meaning: Teaching Comprehension in the Primary Grades* (Miller 2002). Remember that study guides to use as a starting point for your discussions are only a Google click away.

- Plan storytimes for your school-aged patrons. Incorporate strategy instruction with rich, compelling picture books. Encourage readers to recommend books to other readers based on shared connections. Create forms that begin like this:

If you have ever _____, then you might

want to read _____ by

_____ because

_____

_____

_____.

- Create book displays and booklists based on common experiences, like this:

> If you have ever been bullied, then read _____
> _____
> _____
> _____
> _____
> _____.

- Share your connections as you recommend books to readers.

Step 3

Create a Forum for the Arts

- Organize book discussion groups based on visualizing. Have readers choose one or more partners and then self-select a text that lends itself to visualizing. For shorter texts, group members can take turns reading the text aloud and stopping periodically to discuss their questions. For longer texts, group members can agree to a reading schedule and then meet periodically to share and display their visualizations.

- Create an attractive area to display students' sketches and drawings. Showcase the book with children's visualizations.

- Provide materials for students to create puppets or props to reenact their visualizations dramatically.

- Make sure there is an ample supply of blank paper, sticky notes, pencils, markers, colored pencils, and crayons for students to use.

- Make your library not only the showcase for students' visualizations but also their production studio for multimedia interpretations and short videos. Provide access to digital cameras, sound equipment, and video recorders. Create or link to tutorials for PowerPoint, Flash, Adobe Premier, and Windows Movie Maker.

Step 4

Create a Community of Readers through Shared Questions

- Organize book discussion groups based on the questioning strategy. Have readers choose one or more partners and then self-select a text that lends itself to questioning. For shorter texts, group members can take turns reading the text aloud and stopping periodically to discuss their questions. For longer texts, group members can agree to a reading schedule and then meet periodically to discuss their questions.

- Host and monitor question blogs for various genres: mystery, science fiction, fantasy, and historical and realistic fiction.

- Create online book clubs or show your patrons how to join clubs sponsored by public libraries.

- Create self-paced tutorials to show patrons how to use the library's reference resources to answer their "I Wonder . . ." questions.

- Create an eclectic display of fiction books almost guaranteed to provoke questions and then pair the books with related nonfiction titles. For example, pair *The Missing 'Gator of Gumbo Limbo* by Jean Craighead George with *Why Do People Live on the Streets?* by Kaye Stearman; or pair *Alligator* by David Jefferis with *Welcome to the River of Grass* by Jane Yolen.

Step 5

Share Your Expertise with Parents and Teachers

- Collaborate with teachers. School librarians should meet at least monthly with grade-level or content-area teams to co-plan instruction. The collaboration must be scheduled through and supported by school administrators; it should not be the result of hurried conversations in the hall or after school. We have too much to offer and much to learn from our colleagues. Demonstrate the need for shared planning time by presenting to school administrators the results of the numerous studies that show increases in student achievement when library media specialists collaborate with classroom teachers; statistics are readily available through the Library Research Service at http://www.lrs.org. Share Schomberg's

(2003) article describing the benefits of and process for collaboration. Another excellent resource is the PowerPoint presentation by Keith Lance and David B. Loertscher, "Powering Achievement: School Library Media Programs Make a Difference."[3]

- Collaborate with other librarians. Children and young adult librarians should meet at least quarterly with each of the librarians at the schools their branch services; meeting with the school librarians must be considered an essential part of the public library's outreach efforts. There is a subtle divide between public and school librarians, like businesses competing for the same group of consumers—a divide that is evident in the literature and clearly demonstrated by the lack of meaningful collaboration. Assignment alerts, while helpful, should not be the extent of our collaboration, nor should summer reading programs. Each group of librarians has a specialized expertise. For example, my colleagues at the Arbutus Public Library do an outstanding job of engaging children during storytime. Like the other school librarians in our area, I have experience teaching comprehension strategies. The benefits of the two groups sharing their expertise are obvious: engagement and comprehension increase. The collaboration need not necessitate the public librarian visiting every school in his or her branch's service area; instead, it could occur during a potluck dinner or a lunchtime meeting.

- Collaborate with parents. Parents are our patrons' first teachers. As such, they too have a great deal of expertise about what, when, where, how, and why children like to read, yet we seldom solicit their advice. Inviting parents to become members of the school's reading committee, or the public library's advisory board, is an important first step in helping them realize that they are essential partners in creating lifelong readers. The ripple effect of having one active parent with strong community ties on your board or committee is amazing. Information you have been trying to disseminate through fliers for years suddenly becomes part of daily conversations as parents wait to pick up their children from school, dance, or sports. In addition to soliciting parents' advice, we need to communicate clearly what we know about how to create engaged, strategic readers. I have already mentioned that every library should have several circulating copies of 7 *Keys to Comprehension: How to Help Your Kids Read It and Get It!* (Zimmermann and Hutchins 2003). In addition, public and school librarians may want to collaborate to create and deliver to parents workshops that demonstrate through modeling how they can help their children become better readers.

Teaching every child who enters our doors how to "tackle books dotted with multisyllabic words and navigate through trellised sentences that climb across many lines of text" not only ensures that we stay in business but, more important, ensures that every child has equitable access to the wealth of knowledge housed within our walls. In addition, teaching children how to become engaged, strategic readers gives them access to the wealth within but also to the world beyond our walls. Every child can be taught to use comprehension strategies, and every child who is taught how and when to use these strategies will become an actively engaged, strategic reader. As engagement increases, so too will comprehension, resulting in greater engagement in a cycle that I hope is without end. If we join our colleagues whose business is also teaching reading, then I know I can look forward to more not-so-rare-now delicate flowers blossoming into beautiful readers each and every year.

NOTES

1. Because Lansdowne is an elementary school, students are not permitted to bring in music CDs; they can choose to listen only to the library's collection, which is somewhat limited to classical music and kids' songs.
2. None of these suggestions for transforming the physical environment is particularly time-consuming or costly. While I would love to have the comfortable, color-coordinated furniture found in the large chain bookstores, my students prefer inexpensive beanbag chairs, which have the added benefit of being easily disinfected and just as easily relocated when we use our library for meetings. Large stuffed toys, another favorite perch for students as they read, were donated by my daughter—who at age twenty-one is much too old for stuffed toys, or at least so I have tried to convince her. Lamps were also donated, as were the sofa and chairs. Our tables were purchased but are of the inexpensive screw-in-the-legs type found in any large discount store for about $6; we covered them with tablecloths. For less than $150 our library was transformed into a welcoming, cozy environment that invites children to read and discuss books.
3. Available at http://www.lmcsource.com/tech/power/power.htm.

Teaching Comprehension Strategies with Great Books

Connecting

Dependent Readers (preschool and prekindergarten)

Franklin in the Dark, by Paulette Bourgeois

Franklin Says I Love You, by Paulette Bourgeois

Julius, the Baby of the World, by Kevin Henkes

Bread and Jam for Frances, by Russell Hoban

Mama, Do You Love Me? by Barbara M. Joose

The Snowy Day, by Ezra Jack Keats

Chicken Sunday, by Patricia Polacco

Margaret and Margarita / Margarita y Margaret, by Lynn Reiser

Ira Sleeps Over, by Bernard Waber

William's Doll, by Charlotte Zolotow

Emergent Readers (kindergarten through second grade)

Any of the picture books listed above

I Love Saturdays y domingos, by Alma Flor Ada

Fireflies! by Julie Brinckloe

Fly Away Home, by Eve Bunting

Oliver Button Is a Sissy, by Tomie dePaola

Shoes from Grandpa, by Mem Fox

The Good Luck Cat, by Joy Harjo

Tight Times, by Barbara Shook Hazen

Pinky and Rex and the Bully, by James Howe

The Colors of Us, by Karen Katz

The Honest-to-Goodness Truth, by Patricia C. McKissack

Tomas and the Library Lady, by Pat Mora

Thank You, Mr. Falker, by Patricia Polacco

Alexander and the Terrible, Horrible, No Good, Very Bad Day, by Judith Viorst

Alexander, Who Used to Be Rich Last Sunday, by Judith Viorst

Independent Readers (third through eighth grade)

Any of the picture books listed above

My Name is Maria Isabel, by Alma Flor Ada

The Chocolate War, by Robert Cormier

Bud, Not Buddy, by Christopher Paul Curtis

Because of Winn-Dixie, by Kate DiCamillo

Joey Pigza Swallowed the Key, by Jack Gantos

Honey, I Love and Other Love Poems, by Eloise Greenfield

Olive's Ocean, by Kevin Henkes

A Corner of the Universe, by Ann M. Martin

Goin' Someplace Special, by Patricia C. McKissack

Visualizing

Dependent Readers (preschool and prekindergarten)

The Three Billy Goats Gruff (any version)

Mooncake, by Frank Asch

Kitten's First Full Moon, by Kevin Henkes

The Snowy Day, by Ezra Jack Keats

What Do You Do with a Tail Like This? by Robin Page
and Steve Jenkins

My Friend Rabbit, by Eric Rohmann

Cherries and Cherry Pits, by Vera B. Williams

Emergent Readers (kindergarten through second grade)

Any of the picture books listed above

Miss Rumphius, by Barbara Cooney

Ant Cities, by Arthur Dorros

Be Good to Eddie Lee, by Virginia Fleming

Under the Quilt of Night, by Deborah Hopkinson

The Mysterious Tadpole, by Steven Kellogg

Harvesting Hope: The Story of Cesar Chavez,
by Kathleen Krull

Frederick, by Leo Lionni

Snowflake Bentley, by Jacqueline Briggs Martin

Baseball Saved Us, by Ken Mochizuki

Lions at Lunchtime, by Mary Pope Osborne

Spiders, by Carolyn B. Otto

The Keeping Quilt, by Patricia Polacco

Aunt Harriet's Underground Railroad in the Sky,
by Faith Ringgold

Tar Beach, by Faith Ringgold

The Bird House, by Cynthia Rylant

Night in the Country, by Cynthia Rylant

Grandfather Tang's Story: A Tale Told with Tangrams,
by Ann Tompert

Two Bad Ants, by Chris Van Allsburg

Owl Moon, by Jane Yolen

From Tadpole to Frog, by Kathleen Weidner Zoehfeld

Independent Readers (third through eighth grade)

Any of the books listed above

The Children of Green Knowe, by L. M. Boston

The Secret Garden, by Frances Hodgson Burnett

Inkheart, by Cornelia Funke

Pictures of Hollis Woods, by Patricia Reilly Giff

The Wind in the Willows, by Kenneth Grahame

Out of the Dust, by Karen Hesse

The Lion, the Witch, and the Wardrobe, by C. S. Lewis

Journey, by Patricia MacLachlan

Summer Reading Is Killing Me! by Jon Scieszka

Crash, by Jerry Spinelli

Surviving the Applewhites, by Stephanie S. Tolan

Poetry

Gathering the Sun: An Alphabet in Spanish and English, by Alma Flor Ada

The Earth under Sky Bear's Feet: Native American Poems of the Land, by Joseph Bruchac

Spinning through the Universe: A Novel in Poems from Room 214, by Helen Frost

Fold Me a Poem, by Kristine O'Connell George

Honey, I Love and Other Love Poems, by Eloise Greenfield

Fly with Poetry: An ABC of Poetry, by Avis Harley

Calling the Doves / El canto de las Palomas, by Juan Felipe Herrera

Knock at a Star: A Child's Introduction to Poetry, by X. J. Kennedy and Dorothy M. Kennedy

Freedom Like Sunlight: Praisesongs for Black Americans,
  by J. Patrick Lewis

Hailstones and Halibut Bones, by Mary O'Neill

Hoop Queens: Poems, by Charles R. Smith Jr.

Questioning

Dependent Readers (preschool and prekindergarten)

The Grey Lady and the Strawberry Snatcher,
  by Molly Bang

The Snowman, by Raymond Briggs

A Boy, a Dog, and a Frog, by Mercer Mayer

Where the Wild Things Are, by Maurice Sendak

The Polar Express, by Chris Van Allsburg

Tuesday, by David Wiesner

Emergent Readers (kindergarten through second grade)

Any of the picture books listed above

Amelia's Road, by Linda Jacobs Altman

Ruby's Wish, by Shirin Yim Bridges

Fly Away Home, by Eve Bunting

The Lotus Seed, by Sherry Garland

The Storm, by Marc Harshman

Butterfly Boy, by Virginia Kroll

Mr. Lincoln's Way, by Patricia Polacco

The Case of the Marshmallow Monster, by James Preller

The Missing Mummy (A to Z Mystery), by Ron Roy

An Angel for Solomon Singer, by Cynthia Rylant

Henry and Mudge and the Sneaky Crackers,
  by Cynthia Rylant

On the Same Day in March: A Tour of the World's Weather,
   by Marilyn Singer

The Stranger, by Chris Van Allsburg

Freedom Summer, by Deborah Wiles

The Other Side, by Jacqueline Woodson

Independent Readers (third through eighth grade)

Any of the books listed above

Before We Were Free, by Julia Alvarez

The Summer of the Swans, by Betsy Byars

White Socks Only, by Evelyn Coleman*

Walk Two Moons, by Sharon Creech

The Watsons Go to Birmingham—1963,
   by Christopher Paul Curtis

The Missing 'Gator of Gumbo Limbo (Eco Mystery),
   by Jean Craighead George

Who Really Killed Cock Robin? (Eco Mystery),
   by Jean Craighead George

Judy Moody Predicts the Future, by Megan McDonald

Dolphins at Daybreak (Magic Tree House #9),
   by Mary Pope Osborne

Why? by Nikolai Popov*

Holes, by Louis Sachar

Maniac Magee, by Jerry Spinelli

*Although both are considered picture books, thematically the two titles are more appropriate for an older audience.

Finding Answers

Dependent Readers (preschool and prekindergarten)

Allan Fowler

Gail Gibbons

Zoe Hall

Jean Marzollo

Bruce McMillan

Kathleen Weidner Zoehfeld

Emergent Readers (kindergarten through second grade)

Any of the authors listed above

David A. Adler

Aliki

Caroline Arnold

Joanna Cole

Bruce Degen

Betsy Maestro

Bernard Most

Independent Readers (third through eighth grade)

Any of the authors listed above

Jim Arnosky

Isaac Asimov

Arthur Dorros

Ann McGovern

Seymour Simon

Determining Importance

Dependent Readers (preschool and prekindergarten)

>*Red Leaf, Yellow Leaf,* by Lois Ehlert
>
>*The Seasons of Arnold's Apple Tree,* by Gail Gibbons
>
>*The Apple Pie Tree,* by Zoe Hall
>
>*The Dinosaur Who Lived in My Backyard,* by B. G. Hennessy
>
>*I Am an Apple* (Hello Reader Science Level 1), by Jean Marzollo
>
>*A Cat and a Dog,* by Claire Masurel

Emergent Readers (kindergarten through second grade)

>Any of the picture books listed above
>
>*Digging Up Dinosaurs* (Let's-Read-and-Find-Out Science 2), by Aliki
>
>*My Brother Martin: A Sister Remembers Growing Up with the Rev. Dr. Martin Luther King Jr.,* by Christine King Farris
>
>*It's Pumpkin Time!* by Zoe Hall
>
>*Little Blue and Little Yellow,* by Leo Lionni
>
>*Swimmy,* by Leo Lionni
>
>*Swimming with Hammerhead Sharks,* by Kenneth Mallory
>
>*I'm a Seed* (Hello Reader Science Level 1), by Jean Marzollo
>
>*From Seed to Pumpkin* (Let's-Read-and-Find-Out Science 1), by Wendy Pfeffer
>
>*Pumpkin Pumpkin,* by Jeanne Titherington

Independent Readers (third through eighth grade)

>Any of the books listed above
>
>*Come Back, Salmon: How a Group of Dedicated Kids Adopted Pigeon Creek and Brought It Back to Life,* by Molly Cone

Horseshoe Crabs and Shorebirds: The Story of a Food Web,
  by Victoria Crenson

Cells, by Jeanne DuPrau

Julie of the Wolves, by Jean Craighead George

Sarah, Plain and Tall, by Patricia MacLachlan

Martin Luther King, Jr.: Man of Peace,
  by Patricia McKissack and Fredrick McKissack

Heroes, by Ken Mochizuki

Rachel's Journal: The Story of a Pioneer Girl, by Marissa Moss

Earthquake in the Early Morning (Magic Tree House #24),
  by Mary Pope Osborne

Brain and Nerves (Look at Your Body), by Steve Parker

Inferring and Predicting

Dependent Readers (preschool and prekindergarten)

The Mixed-up Chameleon, by Eric Carle

The Very Hungry Caterpillar, by Eric Carle

Monarch Butterfly, by Gail Gibbons

Jillian Jiggs, by Phoebe Gilman

Brown Bear, Brown Bear, What Do You See? by Bill Martin Jr.

If You Give a Pig a Pancake, by Laura Numeroff

What Do You Do with a Tail Like This?
  by Robin Page and Steve Jenkins

There Was an Old Lady Who Swallowed a Fly,
  by Simms Taback

Emergent Readers (kindergarten through second grade)

Any of the picture books listed above

The Number on My Grandfather's Arm,
  by David A. Adler

Arthur's Valentine, by Marc Brown

A River Ran Wild, by Lynne Cherry

Frog and Toad Are Friends, by Arnold Lobel

T Is for Terrible, by Peter McCarty

Tiny the Snow Dog, by Cari Meister

Passage to Freedom: The Sugihara Story,
   by Ken Mochizuki

Amelia Bedelia, by Peggy Parish

A Hat for Minerva Louise, by Janet Morgan Stoeke

Deep in the Forest, by Brinton Turkle

The Bracelet, by Yoshiko Uchida

June 29, 1999, by David Wiesner

Independent Readers (third through eighth grade)

Any of the books listed above

Runaway Ralph, by Beverly Cleary

Sadako and the Thousand Paper Cranes,
   by Eleanor Coerr

And Then There Was One: The Mysteries of Extinction,
   by Margery Facklam

My Side of the Mountain,
   by Jean Craighead George

*You Wouldn't Want to Live in a Wild West Town!
   Dust You'd Rather Not Settle*, by Peter Hicks

Truly Winnie, by Jennifer Jacobson

A Wrinkle in Time, by Madeleine L'Engle

The Sign of the Beaver, by Elizabeth George Speare

The Librarian of Basra: A True Story from Iraq,
   by Jeanette Winter

A Piece of Heaven, by Sharon Dennis Wyeth

Analyzing and Synthesizing

Dependent Readers (preschool and prekindergarten)

> *Cloudy with a Chance of Meatballs*, by Judi Barrett
>
> *Ella Sarah Gets Dressed*, by Margaret Chodos-Irvine
>
> *Miss Rumphius*, by Barbara Cooney
>
> *One Fine Day*, by Nonny Hogrogian
>
> *Harold and the Purple Crayon*, by Crockett Johnson
>
> *The Red Book*, by Barbara Lehman
>
> *Roxaboxen*, by Alice McLerran
>
> *10 Minutes till Bedtime*, by Peggy Rathmann
>
> *My Friend Rabbit*, by Eric Rohmann

Emergent Readers (kindergarten through second grade)

> Any of the picture books listed above
>
> *Hattie and the Wild Waves*, by Barbara Cooney
>
> *Wilfrid Gordon McDonald Partridge*, by Mem Fox
>
> *The Lotus Seed*, by Sherry Garland
>
> *The Man Who Walked between the Towers*, by Mordicai Gerstein
>
> *Alphabet City*, by Stephen T. Johnson
>
> *Three Pigs, One Wolf, and Seven Magic Shapes*, by Grace Maccarone
>
> *Time Flies*, by Eric Rohmann
>
> *The Old Woman Who Named Things*, by Cynthia Rylant
>
> *Math Curse*, by Jon Scieszka
>
> *Science Verse*, by Jon Scieszka
>
> *Grandfather Tang's Story: A Tale Told with Tangrams*, by Ann Tompert

Independent Readers (third through eighth grade)

Any of the books listed above

Chasing Vermeer, by Blue Balliett

Bridges, by Nicola Baxter

The Tale of Despereaux: Being the Story of a Mouse, a Princess, Some Soup, and a Spool of Thread, by Kate DiCamillo

The City of Ember, by Jeanne DuPrau

The Voice That Challenged a Nation: Marian Anderson and the Struggle for Equal Rights, by Russell Freedman

Spinning through the Universe: A Novel in Poems from Room 214, by Helen Frost

Scien-trickery: Riddles in Science, by J. Patrick Lewis

Pyramids, by Fiona Macdonald

American History Fresh Squeezed! 41 Thirst-for-Knowledge-Quenching Poems (Brain Juice), by Carol Diggory Shields

Science Fresh Squeezed! 41 Thirst-for-Knowledge-Quenching Poems (Brain Juice), by Carol Diggory Shields

APPENDIX

Tools
for
Supporting
Strategy
Instruction

Name _____ Date _____

Inferring Meaning with Poetry

Inferring is when readers use their prior knowledge and textual clues to draw conclusions and form unique interpretations of text.

Their tales are long,
Their faces small,
They haven't any
chins at all.
Their ears are pink,
Their teeth are white,
They run about
The house at night.
They nibble things
They shouldn't touch,
And no one seems
To like them much.

What I'm thinking as I read each line:

_____
_____
_____
_____
_____
_____
_____
_____
_____
_____
_____
_____

I'm inferring that . . .

_____
_____
_____
_____
_____

B-1

Name _____ Date _____

Most Important Questions!

Day One

I am reading _____ by

_____.

This is the most important question I want to focus
on tomorrow when I reread the book:

[box]

Day Two

After **rereading** and **focusing** on my question today,
I'm thinking . . .

_____

_____

_____

_____

_____

What **helped** you answer your own question?

_____

_____

_____

B-2

Name _____ Date _____

Title _____

Good readers always make **predictions**
or tell what they think might happen
before reading and as they read!

I predict . . .	What was the *thinking* behind my prediction?
_____	_____
_____	_____
_____	_____
_____	_____
_____	_____
_____	_____
_____	_____
_____	_____
_____	_____
_____	_____
_____	_____
_____	_____
_____	

5 Ws and an H

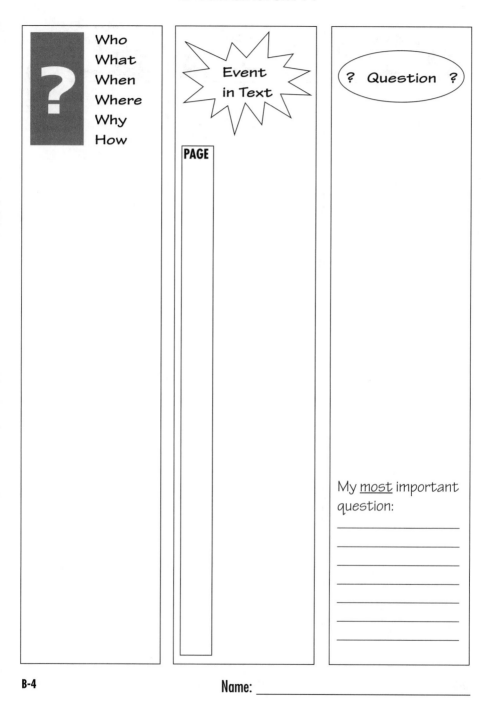

Who
What
When
Where
Why
How

Event
in Text

PAGE

? Question ?

My <u>most</u> important question:

Connections

Text-to-Self	Text-to-Text	Text-to-World

Name: _____

What's the Big Idea?

Summary of the story:

+

What the main character learns:

=

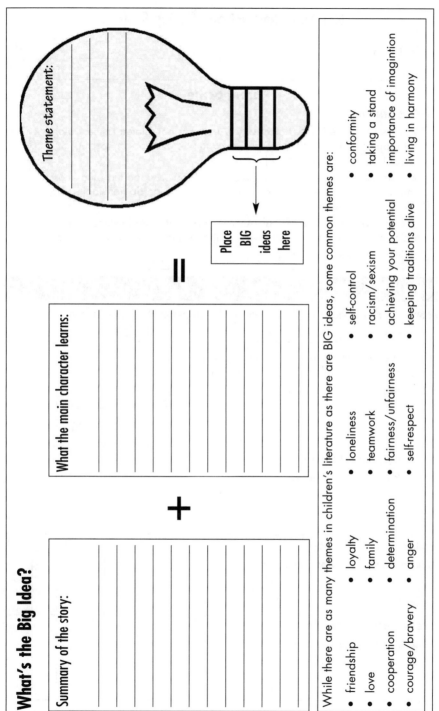

Place
BIG
ideas
here

Theme statement:

While there are as many themes in children's literature as there are BIG ideas, some common themes are:

- friendship
- love
- cooperation
- courage/bravery

- loyalty
- family
- determination
- anger

- loneliness
- teamwork
- fairness/unfairness
- self-respect

- self-control
- racism/sexism
- achieving your potential
- keeping traditions alive

- conformity
- taking a stand
- importance of imagination
- living in harmony

B-6

Name: _____

139

Reading Checklist and Rating Scale

Student's Name: _____

Rating Scale

0 = absent

1 = Incomplete/unsatisfactory (Answer is not related to the topic, or not supported by at least one specific example, or errors in spelling or usage interfere with meaning.)

2 = Satisfactory (Answer is related to the topic, supported by at least one specific example, and errors in spelling or usage do not significantly interfere with meaning.)

3 = Extensive & insightful (Answer is related to and extends the topic, is supported by at least two specific examples, and is free of grammatical and spelling errors.)

BEHAVIORS

Before reading, the student uses information from the title, cover, summary, or about the author to

Make <u>connections</u> to the text based on prior experiences in his or her own life, other texts, or the larger world. *Comments and Dates Assessed*:	0	1	2	3
Pose <u>questions</u> about the text. *Comments and Dates Assessed*:	0	1	2	3
<u>Visualize</u> missing information. *Comments and Dates Assessed*:	0	1	2	3
Make predictions about the text. *Comments and Dates Assessed*:	0	1	2	3

B-7

Set a purpose for reading. *Comments and Dates Assessed:*	0	1	2	3

Makes <u>connections</u> to the text based on prior experiences in his or her own life, other texts, or the larger world. *Comments and Dates Assessed:*	0	1	2	3
Makes meaning by asking and answering <u>questions</u>. *Comments and Dates Assessed:*	0	1	2	3
Merges prior experiences with the text to <u>visualize</u> key details. *Comments and Dates Assessed:*	0	1	2	3
<u>Infers</u> meaning and is able to support inferences with specific examples from the text. *Comments and Dates Assessed:*	0	1	2	3
Uses organizational pattern of text to determine importance. *Comments and Dates Assessed:*	0	1	2	3
Determines importance by discriminating between key topics/themes and supporting details/events. *Comments and Dates Assessed:*	0	1	2	3

B-7

(Cont.)

Uses specific word attack strategies (e.g., context, structural analysis, sound, dictionary). *Comments and Dates Assessed*:	0	1	2	3
Self-corrects and rereads when the text does not make sense. *Comments and Dates Assessed*:	0	1	2	3
Monitors for meaning during oral and silent reading. *Comments and Dates Assessed*:	0	1	2	3
Uses an appropriate reading rate. *Comments and Dates Assessed*:	0	1	2	3
After reading, the student				
Makes <u>connections</u> to the text based on prior experiences in his or her own life, other texts, or the larger world. *Comments and Dates Assessed*:	0	1	2	3
Answers <u>questions</u> and poses new questions to extend meaning. *Comments and Dates Assessed*:	0	1	2	3

B-7

Infers big ideas or themes and supports the inference with specific examples. *Comments and Dates Assessed:*	0	1	2	3
Identifies important topics/themes by determining important ideas and drawing conclusions. *Comments and Dates Assessed:*	0	1	2	3
Synthesizes information by retelling important ideas and links the synthesis to prior knowledge, schema, or texts. *Comments and Dates Assessed:*	0	1	2	3
Judges accuracy, credibility, and logic of text. *Comments and Dates Assessed:*	0	1	2	3
Identifies the basic genre and considers the author's or illustrator's craft. *Comments and Dates Assessed:*	0	1	2	3

B-7

References

Abilock, D. 2004. Commentary. *Knowledge Quest* 33 (2): 8.

ALA (American Library Association). 1998. *Information power: Building partnerships for learning*. Chicago: American Library Association.

———. 2005. Mission. http://www.ala.org/ala/ourassociation/governingdocs/policymanual/mission.htm.

Alpert, B. 1987. Active, silent and controlled discussions: Explaining variations in classroom conversation. *Teaching and Teacher Education* 3:29–40.

Asselin, M. 2002. Comprehension instruction: Directions from research. *Teacher Librarian* 29 (4): 55–58. http://proquest.umi.com/pqdweb? did=116959420.

———. 2004. Guiding the inclusion of information literacy. *Teacher Librarian* 31 (4): 63.

Auger, T. 2003. Student-centered reading: A review of the research on literature circles. *EPS Update* 4 (4): pars. 3–6. http://www.epsbooks.com/flat/newsletter/vol04/iss04/index.asp.

Beers, K. 2002. *When kids can't read: What teachers can do: A guide for teachers 6–12*. Portsmouth, NH: Heinemann.

Buehl, D. 2001. *Classroom strategies for interactive learning*, 2d ed. Newark, DE: International Reading Association.

Busching, B., and B. A. Slesinger. 1995. Authentic questions: What do they look like? Where do they lead? *Language Arts* 72 (5): 341.

CHRPR Committee on Human Rights and Poverty Reduction. 2004. *A conceptual framework*. New York and Geneva: United Nations.

Clark, J. M., and A. Paivio. 1991. Dual coding theory and education. *Educational Psychology Review* 71:64–73.

Cortese, Emma. 2004. The application of Question-Answer Relationship strategies to pictures. *Reading Teacher* 57 (4): 374.

Daniels, H. 2002. Expository text in literature circles. *Voices from the Middle* 9 (4): 7–15. http://proquest.umi.com/pqdweb?did=116914206.

Davis, B. H., V. Resta, L. L. Davis, and A. Camacho. 2001. Novice teachers learn about literature circles through collaborative action research. *Journal of Reading Education* 26:1–6.

Dickson, S. V., D. C. Simmons, and E. J. Kameenui. 1995. Text organization: Curricular and instructional implications for diverse learners. Technical Report No. 1. Eugene, OR: National Center to Improve the Tools of Educators. http://idea.uoregon.edu/~ncite/documents/techrep/tech18.html.

Dillon, J. T. 1988. *Questioning and teaching: A manual of practice.* New York: Teachers College Press.

Eeds, M., and D. Wells. 1989. Grand conversations: An exploration of meaning construction in literature study groups. *Research in the Teaching of English* 23:4–29.

Eisenberg, M. 1998. Tip #5 synthesis: Putting it all together. *Teacher Librarian* 26 (1): 38.

Enciso, P. 1996. Why engagement in reading matters to Molly. *Reading and Writing Quarterly* 12:171–94.

Fader, E. 2003. Deepening the impact. In *How storytimes for preschool children can incorporate current research.* Public Library Association website: http://www.ala.org/ala/pla/plaissues/earlylit/deepeningtheimpact/storytimeapp/storytimeapplications.htm.

Fielding, L. G., and P. D. Pearson. 1994. Reading comprehension: What works. *Educational Leadership* 51 (5): 62–70.

Gambrell, L. B., and P. B. Jawitz. 1993. Mental imagery, text illustrations, and children's story comprehension and recall. *Reading Research Quarterly* 28:264–76.

Graesser, A., J. M. Golding, and D. L. Long. 1991. Narrative representation and comprehension. In R. Barr et al., eds., *Handbook of reading research*, vol. 2, 171–204. White Plains, NY: Longman.

Grimes, S. 2004. The search for meaning. *School Library Journal* 50 (5): 48–53.

Harada, V. H. 2003. Building evidence-based practice through action research. October. http://www2.hawaii.edu/~vharada/vi-Building%20Evidence-12-03-jav.htm.

Harvey, S., and A. Goudvis. 2000. *Strategies that work: Teaching comprehension to enhance understanding.* Portland, ME: Stenhouse.

Keene, E., and S. Zimmermann. 1997. *Mosaic of thought: Teaching comprehension in a reader's workshop.* Portsmouth, NH: Heinemann.

King, C. 2001. I like group reading because we can share ideas: The role of talk with the literature circle. *Reading* 35:32–36.

Koontz, C. 2005. Neighborhood-based in-library use performance measures for public libraries: A nationwide study of majority-minority and majority white/low income markets using personal digital data collectors. *Library and Information Science Research* 27:28–50.

Leu, D. J., Jr. 2000. Our children's future: Changing the focus of literacy and literacy instruction. *Reading Teacher* 53 (5): 424.

Leu, D. J., Jr., M. H. Mallette, and R. A. Karchmer. 2001. New realities, new literacies, and new technologies: Redefining the agenda for literacy research. *Reading Research and Instruction* 40:265–72.

Lyman, P., and H. R. Varian. 2003. How much information, 2003. October 27. http://www.sims.berkeley.edu/how-much-info-2003.

McKenzie, J. 1997. A questioning took kit. *From Now On* 7 (3).

_____. 2000. *Beyond technology: Questioning, research and the information literate school.* Bellingham, WA: FNO Press.

_____. 2001. From trivial pursuit to essential questions and standards-based learning. *From Now On* 10 (5). http://optin.iserver.net/fromnow/feb01/pl.html.

McNamara, D. S., and T. O'Reilly. 2004. Theories of comprehension skill: Knowledge and strategies versus capacity and suppression. In F. Columbus, ed., *Progress in experimental psychology research.* Hauppauge, NY: Nova Science.

McPherson, K. 2004. Visual literacy and school libraries. *Teacher Librarian* 32 (2): 58–60. http://proquest.umi.com/pqdweb?did=761497661.

Miller, D. 2002. *Reading with meaning: Teaching comprehension in the primary grades.* Portland, ME: Stenhouse.

National Endowment for the Arts. 2004. Reading at risk: A survey of literary reading in America. Report No. 46. http://www.arts.gov/pub/ReadingAt Risk.pdf.

National Research Council. 1998. Instructional strategies for kindergarten and the primary grades and Predictors of success and failure in reading. In C. E. Snow, M. S. Burns, and P. Griffin, eds., *Preventing reading difficulties in young children.* Washington, DC: National Academy Press.

NICHD (National Institute of Child Health and Human Development). 2000. *Teaching children to read: An evidence-based assessment of the scientific research literature on reading and its implications for reading instruction.* Comprehension Report of the National Reading Panel. Washington, DC: U.S. Government Printing Office.

Nist, S. L., and M. L. Simpson. 2000. An update on strategic learning: It's more than textbook reading strategies. *Journal of Adolescent and Adult Literacy* 43 (6): 528–42. http://proquest.umi.com/pqdweb?index=0& did=50841994.

Oakhill, J., and N. Yuill. 1986. Pronoun resolution in skilled and less skilled comprehenders: Effects of memory load and inferential complexity. *Language and Speech* 29:25–37.

Paivio, A. 1971. *Imagery and verbal processes.* New York: Holt, Rinehart and Winston.

_____. 1986. *Mental Representations.* New York: Oxford University Press.

Pearson, P. D., and J. A. Dole. 1987. Explicit comprehension instruction: A review of research and a new conceptualization of instruction. *Elementary School Journal* 88:151–65.

Pearson, P. D., and L. Fielding. 1991. Comprehension instruction. In R. Barr et al., eds., *Handbook of reading research*, vol. 2, 815–60. White Plains, NY: Longman.

Pearson, P. D., and D. D. Johnson. 1978. *Teaching reading comprehension*. New York: Holt, Rinehart and Winston.

Pressley, M. 2000. What should comprehension instruction be the instruction of? In M. Kamil et al., eds., *Handbook of reading research*, vol. 3. Mahwah, NJ: Erlbaum.

Pretorius, E. 2000. Reading and the UNISA student: Is academic performance related to reading ability? University of South Africa. http://www.unisa.ac.za.

Raphael, T. E. 1982. Question-answering strategies for children. *Reading Teacher* 36:186–90.

Rieber, L. P. 1994. *Computers, graphics and learning*. Madison, WI: WCB Brown and Benchmark.

Sadoski, M. 1999. Comprehending comprehension. *Reading Research Quarterly* 34 (4): 493–501.

Schomberg, J. 2003. TAG team: Collaborate to teach, assess and grow. *Teacher Librarian* 31 (1).

Seidenberg, P. L. 1989. Relating text-processing research to reading and writing instruction for learning disabled students. *Learning Disabilities Focus* 5 (1): 4–12.

Singer, M. 1988. Inferences in reading comprehension. In M. Daneman, G. E. Mackinnon, and T. G. Waller, eds., *Reading research: Advances in theory and practice*, vol. 6, 177–219. New York: Academic Press.

St. Lifer, E. 2004. Parallel universes. *School Library Journal* 50 (6): 13. http://proquest.umi.com/pqdweb?did=650950961.

Todd, R. J. 2003. School libraries and evidence: Seize the day, begin the future. *Library Media Connection* 22(1): 12. http://proquest.umi.com/pqdweb?index=0&did=428581711.

Tompkins, G. E. 2003. *Literacy for the 21st century*, 3d ed. Upper Saddle River, NJ: Prentice Hall.

Topping, K., et al. 2003. Policy and practice implications of the Program for International Student Assessment (PISA) 2000: Report of the International Reading Association PISA Task Force. http://www.readingonline.org/international/pisa_taskforce/pisa.pdf.

U.S. Department of Education. 2000. Technical report and data file users manual for the 1992 National Adult Literacy Survey. Washington, DC: National

Center for Education Statistics. http://nces.ed.gov/pubsearch/
pubsinfo.asp?pubid=2001457.

Vygotsky, L. 1978. *Mind in society: The development of higher psychological processes.*
Cambridge, MA: Harvard University Press.

Weaver, C. A., III, and W. Kintsch. 1991. Expository text. In R. Barr et al., eds.,
Handbook of reading research, vol. 2, 230–44. White Plains, NY: Longman.

Winne, P. H., L. Graham, and L. Prock. 1993. A model of poor readers' text-
based inferencing: Effects of explanatory feedback. *Reading Research Quarterly*
28 (1): 53.

Yuill, N., and J. Oakhill. 1988. Understanding of anaphoric relations in skilled
and less skilled comprehenders. *British Journal of Psychology* 79 (2): 173–86.

Zabrucky, K., and H. H. Ratner. 1992. Effects of passage type on comprehension
monitoring and recall in good and poor readers. *Journal of Reading Behavior*
24:373–91.

Zimmermann, S., and C. Hutchins. 2003. *7 keys to comprehension: How to help your
kids read it and get it!* New York: Three Rivers Press.

Index

questions appropriate for, 66–67

Internet. *See* Online resources

J

"just right" book. *See* Goldilocks rule

juxtapositions and synthesizing, 103–105, 108–111

K

keyword searching skills, 63, 65, 69, 70, 86

KWL charts, 78

L

layout of text. *See* Text structure and features

learning disabled students and overlays, 99n4

librarians
    collaboration among, 119
    and determining important ideas, 75
    as human resource, 64–65
    and teaching research skills, 62

library sessions, example of, 6–7

M

main idea, identifying, 68–69. *See also* Determining important ideas

modeling of strategies
    analyzing and synthesizing, 105–108
    browsing, 13–15
    determining important ideas, 76–80

drawing, 34
effectiveness of, 4
in fostering engaged reading, 12
inferring and predicting, 96–99
point of view, 36–37
previewing, 3
questioning, 44–48
reading on, 58–60
rereading, 56
selection of reading matter, 14
showing and telling in, 23
skimming, 14, 84
text features and structures, 82–83
text-to-self, 22–27, 28
text-to-text, 28–30
text-to-world connecting, 30–31
time required for, 39
use of directional resources, 65
visualizing, 34–36

mystery books, 45

N

narrative structure, 75–76, 82

Native American cultures exercise, 99–101

newsletters for parents, 12

nonfiction
    determining importance in, 80–85
    visualizing with, 37–39

O

online resources
    evaluation of, 87
    in questioning, 49–50
    reading level, 68–69

overlays, use by students, 99, 101

P

parents
    collaboration with, 119–120
    concerns about reading, 12n5
    newsletters for, 12
    permissions, 17

personal experiences, use of, 24

persuasion, 82

physical environment, 12, 115–116

picture book writing exercise, 111–112

picture books, visualizing with, 36–37

picture or book walk, 14

playground-designing exercise, 104–105

poetry
    reading lists, 124–125
    and visualizing, 39–42
    worksheet, 134

point of view, modeling of, 36–37

posters, 7

poverty and reading, 10–11

predicting. *See also* Inferring
    definition, 3, 95
    worksheets, 135–136

previewing, 3

procedural inferences, 93–94

Q

question-answer relationships (QARs) paradigm, 61

questioning, 43–54. *See also* Answering questions
  categorizing of, 52–53
  and community building, 50–51
  guide practice, 48–50
  and inferring, 91
  modeling of strategies, 44–48
  physical environment for, 118
  reading lists, 125–126
  as reading strategy, 3, 4
Question/Response form, 17–18
questions, essential, 50

R
rain forest exercise, 67–68
readability scales, 68n8
reading comprehension
  measurement of, 74n2
  role of librarian, 1–3
  strategies for, 3–4
  and traditional storytimes, 20–21
reading levels, 68–69, 86
reading lists
  for teaching comprehension strategies, 121–132
  vs. self-selection, 14
reading on as strategy, 58–60, 93
recommendations by students, 115, 116
rereading as strategy, 4, 56–58
resources, use of, 25, 61–71. *See also* Directional resources; Human resources;

Informational resources; Online resources
  background knowledge, 30
  in questioning, 49–50
  tutorials for, 118

S
scaffolded instruction, 4, 17–18
scanning, 85. *See also* Skimming
schema. *See* Background knowledge (schema)
school libraries, justification for, 10
search types, 65, 70
seating in library, 115. *See also* "Crisscross applesauce"
self-check, use of, 24
self-selection of reading matter, 14, 51n5
semantic clues, 82, 84, 93
sensory images, 32–33
sequence, 82
series books, 45
signal words (semantic clues), 82, 84, 93
significance. *See* Determining important ideas
skimming, 14, 84. *See also* Reading on
Sky View Café, 85–86
"Smart Thinking" board, 6
squirming, 77n5
sticky notes, use of, 24, 25
storytimes
  as performance by librarian, 20–21
  and teaching comprehension strategies, 116–117

students as human resources, 63–64
study groups on comprehension, 116
subject tree search technique, 65, 70
summarizing
  in determining important ideas, 80
  using word processing software, 68–69
summary of book in browsing, 14
synthesizing, 4, 103. *See also* Analyzing and synthesizing; Thinking about

T
table of contents, use of, 83. *See also* Text structure and features
tangram exercise, 106–108
teachers, collaboration with, 118–119
text structure and features
  and determining importance, 74, 82–83
  inferring from, 93
  in online text, 87
text supports, 82, 83
text-to-self connecting, 22–27
text-to-text connecting, 27–30
text-to-world connecting, 30–31
thematic inferences, 93
themes, 76, 79
thesauruses, use of, 30, 69–70
think-alouds, 4

thinking about, 60. *See also*
	Inferring;
	Synthesizing
topic sentence, 84
transparencies, use of,
	99–100
tutorials for questioning,
	118

U

uncertainty while reading,
	46n2

V

visualizing, 32–42
	and inferring, 91
	modeling of, 34–36
	nonfiction, 37–39
	physical environment
		for, 117
	picture books, 36–37
	poetry, 39–42
	reading lists for,
		122–124

as reading strategy, 3
vocabulary building
	inferring from
		context, 93, 100
	and poetry, 40–42
	and word processing
		software, 69–70

W

War on Poverty, 10
water quality exercise,
	108–111
"What's the Big Idea"
	handout, 80–81, 139
Winfrey, Oprah, 11
Wonder Books/Boxes/
	Cards, 50
word processing software
	as scaffold, 8
	in text-to-world con-
		necting, 30–31
	in use of informa-
		tional resources,
		68–70

and vocabulary,
	40–42, 69–70
worksheets and forms
	5 Ws and an H, 137
	Connections, 4, 138
	"I wonder" log, 48–49
	"I wondered as I was
		reading" (Ques-
		tion/Response), 17
	Inferring Meaning
		with Poetry, 134
	Most Important
		Questions!,
		135–136
	Reading Checklist
		and Rating Scale,
		140–143
	What's the Big Idea?
		80–81, 139
writing as synthesis,
	111– 112

Sharon Grimes is School Library Media Specialist at Lansdowne Elementary in Baltimore County. She was named Baltimore County Teacher of the Year for 2004–5 and Technology Educator of the Year for 2003–4. The Baltimore Sun recognized her efforts in enabling every child to become a reader by nominating her for its Reading by 9 All-Star award. She is the author of numerous online research models and the article "The Search for Meaning" (School Library Journal, May 2004). Grimes earned her master's in information technology from Towson University and is pursuing her PhD in language, literacy, and culture at the University of Maryland–Baltimore County.